D1129806

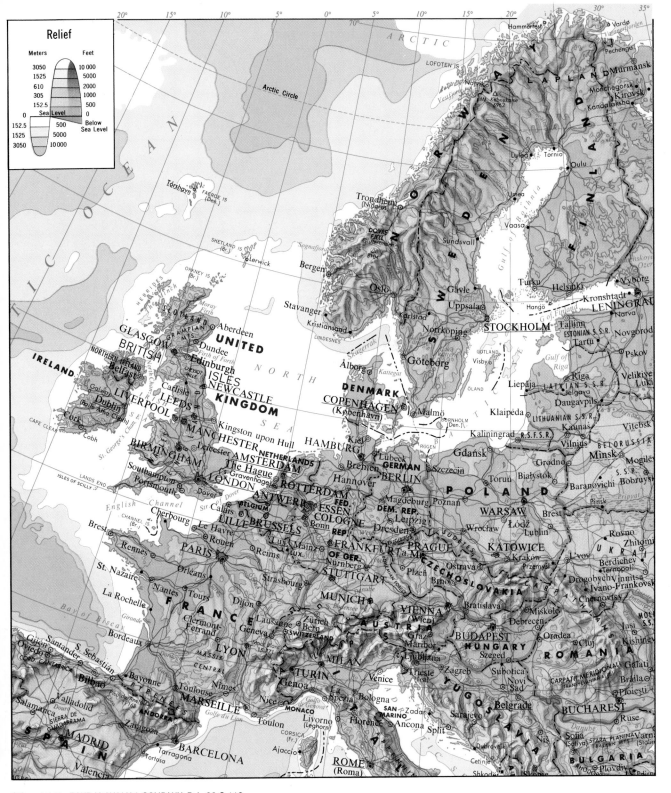

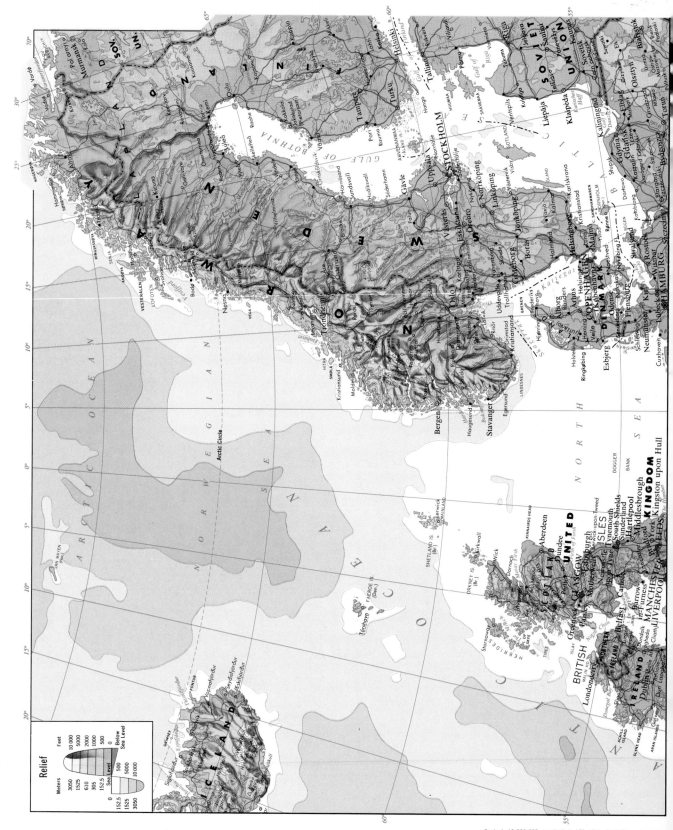

Scale 1: 10 000 000; one inch to 160 miles. Conic Projection
Elevations and depressions are given in feet

Enchantment of the World

NORWAY

By Martin Hintz

Consultant: Ed Conradson, Director, Norwegian Information Center, New York

Consultant for Social Studies: Donald W. Nylin, Ph.D., Assistant
Superintendent for Instruction, Aurora West Public Schools, Aurora, Illinois

Consultant for Reading: Robert L. Hillerich, Ph.D., Bowling Green State
University, Bowling Green, Ohio

CHILDRENS PRESS, CHICAGO

*The Troll Path
(Trollstigen)
in Romsdal*

For Louis Larson, my great-grandfather, who was one of those thousands of sturdy Norwegians who left the security and comforts of home to find a new life in the United States. He was a philosopher, a dreamer, a gentleman.

Many thanks are extended to the Norwegian National Tourist Office, the Royal Norwegian Ministry of Foreign Affairs, the Norwegian-American Chamber of Commerce, the Norwegian consulate staff, the Norwegian Information Service, the cooks, bakers, and other kitchen staff at Milwaukee's Immanuel Lutheran Church, and Mr. Bent Vanberg of the International Headquarters of the Sons of Norway. Their help, advice, and suggestions in the preparation of this book were valuable, appreciated, and welcomed.

Library of Congress Cataloging in Publication Data

Hintz, Martin.
  Norway.

  (Enchantment of the world)
  Includes index.
  Summary: Describes the people, culture, geography, history, and economy of the Scandinavian country that is divided in half by the Arctic Circle.
  1. Norway—Juvenile literature. [1. Norway]
I. Title. II. Series.
DL411.H56 1982   948.1   82-9400
ISBN 0-516-02780-8   AACR2

Picture Acknowledgments

Colour Library International: Cover, pages 4, 6, 23, 28, 34, 36, 37, 40, 41, 50, 52, 54, 55, 57, 59, 60, 62, 63, 64, 65, 67, 70 (top), 72, 73, 90, 93, 108, 123
Floyd Johnson, Artist, Floyd Johnson Studio, Minneapolis, Minnesota: Pages 5, 9, 12, 13, 15, 16 (left), 17, 117
The Norwegian Information Service in the United States: Pages 10, 38, 42, 48, 49, 58 (bottom), 66, 69, 70 (bottom left and right), 74, 77, 81, 85, 86, 88, 89, 92, 95, 96, 98
Historical Pictures Service, Inc., Chicago: Pages 11, 14, 16 (right), 19, 20, 21, 25, 26, 29
UPI: Page 32
The Museum of Science and Industry, Chicago: Page 45
Norwegian National Tourist Office: Pages 51, 58 (top), 94, 97, 101, 102
Chicago Stadium: Page 78
Tom Dunnington, Artist: Page 105
Reidar Rosenvinge, Chicago: Page 111
Len Meents: Maps on pages 18, 58, 62, 63, 64, 65, 66, 67
Courtesy Flag Research Center, Winchester, Massachusetts 01890: Flag on back cover
Cover: This scene near Balestrand typifies much of Norway's scenery.

Norwegian Viking,
"Standing Tall"

TABLE OF CONTENTS

Chapter 1   The Folk of the North (Prehistory to Present). 7

Chapter 2   Today's Vikings (Everyday Life). 35

Chapter 3   Nature's Rock-Tossed Playground (Geography). 53

Chapter 4   Sporting in a Rugged Country (Sports). 75

Chapter 5   Land of Caring (Government, Health and Welfare, Education). 79

Chapter 6   A Nation of Achievers (Agriculture and Industry). 91

Chapter 7   Some Famous Norwegians. 99

Chapter 8   Folktales, Music, Art, and Literature. 104

Mini-Facts at a Glance. 114

Index. 123

Hauk's view of the Western Sea from his lookout point on the cliff would have been much like this scene at modern-day Haugesund.

Chapter 1

THE FOLK OF THE NORTH

The rocks crown the Western Sea, that wide, rolling spread of water that meets the horizon. White foam caps the waves, looking like troll hats in the distance. The wind is still raw and cold this morning as it whistles in from the ocean. Morning creeps out of the sky while Hauk stands at the edge of the cliff. He clutches his red cape tightly about his body and peers into the distance.

Today should be the day when the dragon ships come home. Hauk's father, Erik, is captain of one of these mighty *karfi*. The Viking war vessels had sailed away many months ago. Led by Haakon the Longbeard, the fleet had left for its yearly raid on the faraway islands of Britain. Hauk was too young to go on that voyage. But he feels certain he will be ready next year.

For the past several weeks, Hauk has been on the lookout point. He has been keeping watch for the returning ships. He hurries out each morning before the seabirds are awake, hoping to see those first billowing sails. Hauk longs to be one of his father's warriors. For the past year, he has been practicing his swordsmanship. The old veteran who oversees the military training of the village's young men has been helping him. Hauk has made good progress. It has been a long time since his father has watched his son in action. The boy knows Erik will be proud of him.

A week ago, a Scottish *thrall* (slave) had run up the inland road near the sea. He had brought exciting news. The dragon ships had been sighted far off the southernmost islands. Soon they should be nearing the *fjord* (inlet) near Hauk's village. But it is very hard for Hauk to wait.

It is the same for Ingrid, Hauk's younger sister. She is just as eager to see her father. Ingrid often joins her brother at his windy outpost, but not until she has finished her tasks at home. Somehow baking bread doesn't seem as exciting as a voyage to Ireland or to the far settlements in Iceland. Someday, she dreams, she would even like to sail to the distant lands of Arabia or into the Black Sea. She has heard about these places from the wandering *skald,* the minstrel who sometimes visits the village. Ingrid loves to listen to his wondrous tales about the wide world. But then she always has to go back to sewing, salting fish, and taking care of the family goats. Definitely not exciting, she thinks.

This morning, Ingrid joins Hauk on the rocks, though she must be back home by midday. Excitedly, the two young people look toward the place they know the Viking ships will first appear.

Suddenly, there they are! Squinting into the distance, Ingrid and Hauk spot the first huge sail rearing over the waves. The splotch of red against the gray-green sea grows larger and larger as a ship approaches. Following closely are more sails, more masts, more of the long-bodied ships. The flashing oars dig deeply into the ocean, giving another burst of speed. The sailors are eager to be home. The dragon ships with their beautifully carved bows soon fill the far reach of the fjord. Their decks are crammed with raiding booty. Ingrid and Hauk dash back down the path toward their village, shouting happily. Erik's ship is near the head of the fleet, as always, where it should be. Their father is home.

Viking fleets like this one sailed from fjords all along the coast of Norway.

This scene might be typical of what you would see by using your imagination and looking back nine hundred years to early Norway. Many young persons like Hauk and Ingrid eagerly watched for Viking fleets that had sailed from the fjords and safe ports all along the rugged Norwegian coast. Hauk and Ingrid would not have called themselves Norwegian, however. That name would come much, much later. But they knew they were part of a mighty nation of explorers, warriors, and tradespeople who were spreading their influence throughout much of the known world.

Many rock carvings made during the Bronze Age depicted ships like the ones shown here.

THE EARLIEST SETTLERS

Even before the ancient Vikings stormed out of their northern hideaways to "see the world" and conquer, there were people in what is today's Norway. Most of them were hunters and fishermen, rather than bold warriors. These people settled in the land more than ten thousand years ago. Numerous rock carvings have been found, probably made by these Stone Age people before their hunting expeditions. Whales, birds, elk, fish, and reindeer dance across the walls of caves or over rocky cliff facings. Historians say that the carvings were probably magical in meaning, so the hunters or fishermen would be assured of a good kill or catch.

Later, during the Bronze Age, men began to use metal tools. Bronze Age carvings included ships. Much of Norse mythology—the tales told by the skalds—might have begun during this time.

The chief Viking god, Odin

Gradually, however, the early peaceful settlers were displaced. They may have been overrun by more-powerful invaders. Or they may have been swallowed up by warlike neighbors who wanted decent farming land. The change in the people can be traced by observing the change in their gods. The hunting, fishing, and farming spirits were edged out by rough types who threw thunderbolts and demanded bloody sacrifices. The evil deities were the *jotners*. The good spirits—usually more powerful—were called *aeser*.

THE NEW GODS

Chief among these new gods was Odin. He was nicknamed "The Fury," which gives a hint about his temper. Odin was surrounded in the heavens by a court of other Viking gods. They supposedly spent their time making thunderstorms. One of the best known of these spirits was Thor. He was the son of Odin and always carried a big hammer. The Vikings feared their gods, but they also respected them. It was a great honor for a Viking to die in battle. That meant his soul would be carried to Odin's court at Valhalla.

11

Viking ships like these were shallow-draft boats that could maneuver in almost any kind of water.

THE CONQUERING VIKINGS

The Vikings came from a larger region than what is now Norway. They came from villages and fortified military camps all over Scandinavia, which includes present-day Sweden and Denmark. One reason they were feared was that they were excellent seafarers. Their shallow-draft boats could go far inland on any river that connected with the sea. Nothing seemed safe from their raids. The Vikings stormed southward along the coast of western Europe and eastward toward the Black Sea and what is now Russia. They even sailed through the Strait of Gibraltar and into the Mediterranean area.

Viking men and women were farmers, traders, fishermen, boatbuilders, goldsmiths, ironworkers, and artists, as well as excellent seafarers.

Most of the Viking people probably were not the wild men portrayed in legend. Recent historians have claimed that many Vikings lived quietly, as farmers or traders. The ancient Norsemen, as they were sometimes called, were expert boatbuilders, goldsmiths, ironworkers, and artists. But Scandinavia's geography forced its people to use the sea. There was no other way to reach the thousands of offshore islands or visit other communities along the coastline. There weren't many roads over mountains, so a journey by sea was often the safest and easiest way to get around. While they were sailing about, the Vikings may have gotten carried away with the spirit of adventure. They sailed on and on, discovering Iceland, Greenland, and North America. Their settlements stretched across the northern rim of the world, and the Viking culture seeped in everywhere.

Brian Boru and his Irish warriors just before they defeated the Viking armies at Clontarf, outside of Dublin

Many of the wandering Vikings eventually made their homes in the areas they had raided. They mingled with the local populations and often adopted their customs, language, and habits. An area in western France was eventually called Normandy. It was named for the Norsemen who put away their sea chests and weapons to become respectable neighbors.

It wasn't so pleasant elsewhere, however. There was constant warfare between the Vikings and the Irish. Attacks from the north came as early as A.D. 820. "The seas washed flows of strangers over Erin and there was no place and no protection against Vikings and pirates," according to the famous ancient Irish writings called the *Ulster Annals.*

In 836, the Vikings conquered Dublin, which became the seat of Norse power in Ireland. But over the generations, the gentle Irish rains—and the fierce Irish warriors themselves—melted the tough Viking spirit. In 1036, the Irish under Brian Boru defeated the Viking armies at Clontarf outside of Dublin.

This painting depicts the discovery of Greenland by Eric the Red. Note the Viking ship in the lower left-hand corner.

The Vikings were true pioneers, filled with adventurous spirit. They were independent as well, always looking toward the next frontier. When Iceland became crowded, Eric the Red led colonists to Greenland. It was from that huge island that Viking sailors set out to find another new world. They discovered it in Newfoundland, on the coast of North America. On this new continent, there were no fabled riches as in Europe. There were only native Americans, called *skraelings* by the Vikings.

But the new settlements never lasted long. The colonies were too far apart to be supplied adequately. Besides, the skraelings and the Eskimo tribes on Greenland weren't friendly. They often killed Viking settlers who wandered too far afield. The last major voyages to these regions were in the eleventh century. Some Viking outposts were maintained for another generation, however. So there was still some contact with this New World well before Christopher Columbus's famous voyage.

Far left: A Viking sailor hoists the sail.
Left: The Oseberg dragon head, found with a buried Viking ship, is similar to a Viking figurehead.
Opposite: A Viking helmsman navigates his open ship in rough seas. During storms, a tent protected the crew. As he rowed, each man would sit on a trunk containing his personal gear.

Traders were very important in Viking society. Kaupang, near Oslo Fjord in Norway, was a major commercial center in the 800s. Trading contacts even then were being made throughout the British Isles and along the North Sea coasts.

Archaeologists have found numerous artifacts on the site of the old city. They show how widespread the trading was in those days. But by A.D. 975, Kaupang had become less important because other trading centers had emerged in Norway, Sweden, and Denmark.

The Vikings covered an amazing amount of territory. Their ships were never more than 77 feet (23.5 meters) long. They made long voyages without the aid of a compass, in vessels powered only by oars and a single sail. Shields would be hung over the sides of a ship during battles. The figurehead—the wooden figurine at the prow or front of the ship—was usually in the shape of a dragon.

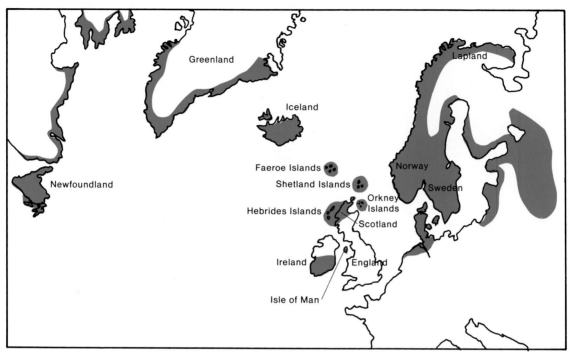

The ancient kingdom of Norway about A.D. 950

These Norwegians, these early Vikings, were members of clans who joined together for raids under the leadership of an important local warrior. As the years went on, a political system developed—stronger warrior chiefs defeated the others. The first Norwegian strong man of this type was Harald Fair Hair.

From 872 to 940, Harald ruled with an iron fist. He made treaties with chiefs all over the North or took their land in battle. When he died, Harald left a royal line of succession with an assortment of good and bad leaders. Among them were the likes of Erik Bloody Axe, Harald Gray Fur, and Magnus the Blind.

This ancient kingdom of Norway was about twice as large as modern Norway. It included parts of Sweden, the Faeroe Islands, Iceland, Greenland, Newfoundland, large chunks of Ireland, the Isle of Man, the Hebrides Islands, northern Scotland, the Orkneys, the Shetland Islands, and much of the Lapp territories in the far north. But it was a shaky kingdom that needed constant attention.

Olav Tryggvason (above) tried to introduce Christianity to Norway in the late 900s. Olav Haraldson (left), who firmly established Christianity, became the patron saint of Norway.

Religion was always important to a Norseman. He truly enjoyed his old rough and tough gods. For years, the Vikings had bumped heads with the Christian nations to the south. For a long time they preferred burning churches to attending them. It wasn't until the time of Olav Tryggvason (Olav I), who became a Christian in England, that the "White Christ" began to be accepted by these rugged people. Olav was the first king since Harald Fair Hair to bring Norway under firm control. He tried to introduce Christianity into his nation in the late 900s.

A TIME OF CONFUSION

But the old gods were powerful and didn't give up easily. After a couple of petty earls ruled Norway, Olav Haraldson (Olav II) tried to make order out of the situation. This Olav, however, was deposed by the pagan King Knut of the twin kingdoms of Denmark and England. Olav II was killed when he tried to regain his throne. Yet Olav became the symbol of Norway's national unity and eventually was named the patron saint of the country.

Harold of England died with an arrow in his eye at the Battle of Hastings in 1066.

The Danes and the Norwegians finally made peace in 1038. To cement the new friendship, there was handshaking all around and the drinking of the powerful alcoholic beverage called *mead.* Almost as soon as the mead ran out, however, both countries were at each other's throats again. The tough Norwegian chieftain, Harald Hardrade, took control. He founded Oslo (now the Norwegian capital) between arguments with his neighbors.

After picking a fight with his cousin, Harold of England, Harald Hardrade was killed in the Battle of Stamford Bridge in 1066. Thus ended Viking attempts to take over all of England. That victory wasn't much comfort to the English Harold. Within days after he defeated the Norwegians, his country was attacked by Normans from France. They were descendants of the Norwegian Vikings who had settled on the continent years earlier. Poor Harold died with an arrow in his eye at the famous Battle of Hastings and the Normans moved in permanently. Thus did the Norwegians indirectly get their revenge.

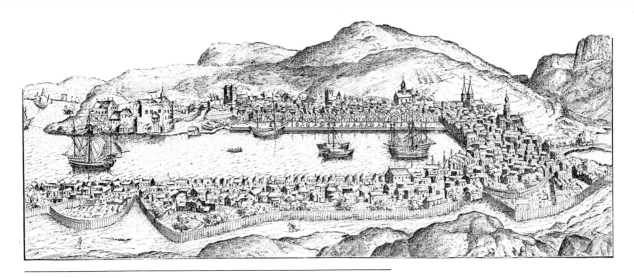

The city of Bergen, shown above in the sixteenth century, was established by Magnus II and Olav the Peaceful in 1070.

Harald Hardrade's sons, Magnus II and Olav the Peaceful, stayed home. But they were like their father in one respect. They built cities. Bergen was established in 1070, followed soon after by Stavanger. Both are important Norwegian communities today.

However, with the death of Sigurd I in 1130—the last of the descendants of Harald Fair Hair—a long period of darkness and confusion settled over Norway. No one ruled the country very well. Sometimes it was hard to tell who was the true king.

All sorts of pretenders to the Norwegian crown appeared. Many of them claimed to be illegitimate, lost sons of King Magnus Bareleg, who was the grandson of Olav III. Imagine how confused the Norwegian peasants felt. They hardly knew from one day to the next who their ruler was. But both the church and the traders took advantage of this political confusion and gained more power. Trade boomed, especially with Britain, and the cities prospered. Merchants from the Hanseatic League—a string of powerful, independent cities in northern Europe—cornered the grain market. They traded grain for Norwegian fish. Since no one knew who was in charge, many minor officials began to run the day-to-day operations of the country.

A BLACK DEATH

By 1217, some stability had returned to the throne, with the coronation of King Haakon IV. His reign was a bright spot in an otherwise troubled century in Norway. He ruled until 1263, and was followed by his son, King Magnus the Lawmaker. Under Magnus, medieval Norway flourished. Many cathedrals were built and a central system of laws was created. Finally, peace seemed to be settling over the countryside. Magnus's son, Haakon V, made Oslo the capital of Norway.

This calm did not last long. Norway was ravaged by the Black Plague, a horrible disease that swept across Europe. In the middle of the fourteenth century, almost half the Norwegian population of 350,000 died miserably.

The plague affected rich and poor, nobles and peasants. To make things even worse, famine swept over Norway and thousands died.

THE DANISH RULE

Through marriage, many foreigners entered the country, especially from Denmark. So it was almost by default that the power in Norway soon passed to that country. The Hanseatic merchants controlled most of the trade. Danish rulers adopted a royal charter that gave them Norway. The Norwegian governing council, the *ting*, was abolished. And the Danish king forced the Protestant Lutheran Reformation on the Norwegian Catholics.

The Norwegians preferred to remain with the traditional Catholic Church. But the loyal bishops and priests were forced to flee Norway. The people thus lost another important part of their Norwegian heritage.

The stave (wooden) Borgund church is a beautiful example of the ornately carved churches built in Norway during the eleventh and twelfth centuries.

Under Denmark, Norway became involved in that nation's wars. Since Denmark was not very successful in military endeavors, she lost more than she gained. Norway was forced to give up a lot of hard-won Viking territory to the Swedes. It became a land that looked much as it does on today's maps.

Eventually, Norway was left alone except by Danish tax collectors. Norway became a trading power, and many of her ships sailed all over the world. Also during this time most farmers were allowed to operate their own farms. No longer did they have to act as tenants for large landowners.

Yet during the Napoleonic Wars in the 1800s, Norway suffered again. Denmark was allied with Napoleon of France against almost all of the rest of Europe. Norway, of course, had to go along with her ruling power. Norway was blockaded and many of her people starved. When Napoleon was defeated, Denmark was supposed to pay for her part in the conflict. By the Treaty of Kiel, the defeated Danes gave to Sweden their rights over Norway because the Swedes had fought with the winning side. Thus ended four hundred years of Danish rule over Norway.

The Norwegians objected to a treaty over which they had had no control. A movement for independence was beginning to grow.

The Danish crown prince, Christian Frederik, was ambitious. He didn't want to see Norway, part of his inheritance, slip away under the new treaty. He took advantage of this international confusion and went to Norway to urge the people to support him as their king.

But he discovered that although the Norwegians didn't care much for the Swedes, they did not really want a Dane back in power. Besides, there were some rumors that England would help Norway become independent.

The elected representatives shown here wrote the Norwegian constitution at Eidsvoll in 1814.

THE SWEDISH RULE

Several of the country's leading citizens went to an estate near the town of Eidsvoll in eastern Norway in the spring of 1814. There they considered Christian Frederik's proposal. They convinced him to call for elections to name delegates to a general assembly. Norwegians went to their churches to vote and swore to defend their country. The representatives who were elected then went to Eidsvoll to work on a constitution.

Danish Crown Prince Christian Frederik (left) was king of Norway for less than six months in 1814.

It took five weeks for the representatives to write the document. Many of their ideas of liberty and freedom were based on parts of the United States and Spanish constitutions. The document was signed on May 17, 1814. The date is now celebrated as Norwegian Independence Day. On the same day, Christian Frederik got his wish. He was crowned king of Norway.

So Norway had a brand-new king, a fine constitution, and a democratically elected parliament. The parliament was called the Storting. The Swedes, however, considered this activity to be revolutionary. And they certainly didn't like a Dane to be calling himself king of Norway. So they declared war. It was a short war, lasting only eighteen days. The Norwegians fought well, but they didn't have enough military power to match their Swedish neighbors. A peace was declared.

Under a new treaty, a compromise was reached. Norway accepted a union with Sweden, with the Swedish king as ruler of both countries. The Norwegians, however, were permitted to keep their new constitution. On November 4, the Storting accepted the plan and elected Swedish King Carl XIII to be king of Norway. That left Christian Frederik without a kingdom. He went back home to Denmark.

Of course, the peace wasn't as calm as it seemed. Under the provisions of the Treaty of Kiel, Norway was still supposed to pay for part of Denmark's national debt. Since Norway was no longer part of that country, the Norwegians naturally didn't want to pay.

Another basic problem between the two countries concerned representation abroad. Under the union, Norwegian foreign relations were handled by the Swedish king and his cabinet in Stockholm.

These difficulties were eventually resolved. Norwegians, however, maintained a strong desire to be totally independent. Under the union, Norway experienced massive growth in its economy, culture, and social systems. The population almost tripled between 1814 and 1900. It grew from about 880,000 to 2 million, even though many Norwegians left the country during this period. Most of them went to the United States. (Next to Ireland, no other European nation lost so many of its people to America. Some 800,000 Norwegians had moved to the United States by the 1920s.)

The timber forests of Norway were as valuable in the nineteenth century as they are today.

Norway's timber was in great demand, as were its fish, textiles, and dairy products. The Norwegian merchant fleet continued to expand. Steamships replaced sailing vessels. The trading tradition of the Vikings remained strong. Some merchants in Sweden tried to gain control of Norway's trade. Commerical competition caused the most trouble between the two countries.

AN INDEPENDENT NATION

In 1905, the Storting voted to set up separate Norwegian consulates. These would be offices around the world to help Norwegian citizens in foreign countries with trade problems and other matters. The Swedish king, Oscar II, vetoed that decision. This caused Norwegian representatives in Stockholm to resign. The king refused to accept the resignations and the dispute threatened to become violent. On June 7, 1905, the Storting bravely said that the union between Sweden and Norway was dissolved. King Oscar decided to accept the situation.

*In 1905, Norwegians marched in the streets (left) to demonstrate their desire
for independence from Sweden. Prince Carl of Denmark agreed to be king
of an independent Norway and became Haakon VII (right) in 1905. He was
eighty-five when he died in 1957, the world's oldest and longest-reigning monarch.*

In a vote, the Norwegians supported the separation. The official
tally was 368,208 for and only 184 against. It was a landslide cry
for independence and the Norwegians danced in the streets.

Now there came a search for a new king. The Norwegians
certainly didn't want another Swede. They looked all over for a
likely candidate. Prince Carl of Denmark agreed to take the job if
the Norwegians wanted him. They did, voting overwhelmingly to
make Carl their leader. He took the name King Haakon VII at his
coronation in 1905.

Although the Norwegians liked the idea of a king, some of them felt Haakon was too stuffy and too Danish. He wasn't accepted socially at first, at least in political circles. But Haakon went his own way and made friends among the common people. He was quiet and reserved and kind. He was also a skilled diplomat.

In 1907, Great Britain, France, Russia, and Germany signed a treaty with Norway. At last she was truly a nation. The treaty made it official in the eyes of the international community.

THE UNDERGROUND WAR

When World War I erupted in 1914, Norway remained neutral. The country traded with both sides during that war. Many Norwegians made fortunes, at least in the opening years of the conflict. Industry boomed, shipping expanded. Then the horrors started. Many of Norway's ships were sunk by submarines and the British blockaded Germany, halting trade.

The war finally ground to a bloody end. The Norwegian fishing industry had to be rebuilt and the country owed money to almost everyone. To make things even worse, Norway was hit very hard as the Great Depression swept the world. It was like the Black Plague, only this disease affected the economy. Everyone had a hard time finding jobs and enough to eat. Labor unrest was a big problem in Norwegian factories and strikes were common. But slowly, by the middle 1930s, Norway gradually began to recover.

In Germany, Adolf Hitler's Nazis were making threats against the world. Norway again claimed to be neutral. On September 1, 1939, Germany invaded Poland and World War II began. Despite her protests, the war came to Norway. The sea-lanes around the country were important, and many battles were fought in the area. Then, on April 9, 1940, the Nazis invaded under the pretext of defending the Norwegians from British attack. Of course, the Norwegians knew better and prepared to fight. But it didn't take long before the Germans took control of the nation. King Haakon and most of the government leaders were forced to flee to England.

There they set up a government in exile and established an underground, or secret force, back home to continue the fight. The Nazis tried to establish their own government in Norway. Their few Norwegian supporters were led by a former defense minister, Vidkun Quisling. Quisling was an admirer of Hitler and had many German Nazi friends. This man was so hated by the Norwegians that the word *quisling* now means "traitor." The Nazis never were able to exert much control over the angry Norwegians, who resisted them everywhere.

Schools were closed because teachers and students refused to pay attention to the Nazi doctrines. Almost 35,000 Norwegians were arrested by the Germans. Many were sent to concentration camps in Norway or Germany. But the Norwegians continued to resist. In London, King Haakon and his son, Crown Prince Olav, helped coordinate the war effort for Norway.

Luckily, the Norwegian merchant fleet was not captured by the Germans. It was used by the Allies (the anti-German nations) to carry supplies all over the world. Norwegians who had escaped the German invaders were trained by the English. Even neutral Sweden helped out. Many Norwegians fled to that country. Men and boys enrolled in Swedish camps that trained policemen, dreaming of the day they could return home to fight for their country. Youngsters who stayed in Norway fled to the mountains to escape being drafted into a labor force by the Germans.

A scowling Vidkun Quisling, whose name now means "traitor" in all languages, is shown the day before he went on trial for World War II war crimes in Norway.

In Norway, the Germans didn't understand why the people didn't welcome them. Norwegians wouldn't even sit next to Germans on a bus. The Norwegians had always hated conquerors, and they loved freedom and independence. No invading Nazi was going to tell a Norwegian what he or she must or must not do or believe. The Germans set up Quisling as prime minister, but he was so unpopular that he had to resign a few days later. Eventually, the Nazis put him back in power. He was supported by the Gestapo, the feared and hated Nazi secret police. But even then, the ordinary Norwegian paid no attention to him.

Many Norwegian soldiers returned secretly to Norway to conduct their underground war. They blew up military installations, power plants, and other services needed by the Germans. Some of these adventures later were used as plots for famous movies and books.

Eventually, the war turned against the Nazis. Soon they were losing on all fronts. The liberation of Norway began in 1944. The Soviet army chased the Germans out of neighboring Finland into the far northern reaches of Norway, called Finnmark.

The Germans retreated southward, burning everything in their path. For a time, it was thought that the Nazis would gather in Norway for their final stand. But that didn't happen and the Germans surrendered all their troops in Europe in May, 1945. A few days later, Prince Olav returned to Norway to the rejoicing of his people. On June 7, his father, King Haakon, came back. On that same date, five years earlier, he had flown into exile.

Quisling and twenty-four other Norwegians who had helped the Nazis were executed after a trial. Freedom ruled again.

After the war, Norway had to reconstruct most of its industry, communications, and other services needed to run the country. The nation received a great deal of monetary help from the United States under the famous Marshall Plan. This was an economic program that many war-torn countries used to rebuild themselves. Reconstruction was completed by the 1950s.

The war years were difficult for the Norwegians but they carried through with their typical bravery and spirit.

Most Norwegians live near the mountains or by the sea, which they call "the blue meadow."

Chapter 2

TODAY'S VIKINGS

By the 1980s, Norway's population reached about five million. But who are the Norwegians? Basically, the Norwegians are people who have been shaped by the land they live in. They are proud of their country because it took hundreds of years to attain their freedom. They guard that freedom fiercely.

The Norwegians have plenty of room to stretch. Most of them live by the sea, which they call the "blue meadow," or near the mountains. About 40 percent of the people live in or around the capital, Oslo. That city is in the southeastern part of the nation, not far from the Swedish border. Norwegians love the outdoors. Their cities have plenty of parks for strolling, picnicking, ball playing, and simply loafing.

There really are no slums in Norway, because most of the housing has been built since the end of World War II. Homes are very efficient and modern, with the style of architecture setting trends around the world. Many Norwegians live in blocks of apartments. About half the families in Norway own their own homes.

This Lapp family of Finnmark is dressed in colorful, traditional clothing.

THE PEOPLE

Most Norwegians are from the same ethnic background. The typical Norwegian is tall and blond, with a narrow face, and eyes that are usually blue or gray.

Some shorter, darker Norwegians live in the southern part of the country. They may be descendants of thralls brought to the country by Vikings generations ago. Yet the only true racial minority among the Norwegians are the Lapps (the Samis). Most Lapps live in Finnmark, the far northern region of the country. The Lapps have Oriental features, dark hair and eyes, and are much shorter than their countrymen.

The Lapps belong to a tribal system that extends through all of Scandinavia and on into Russia. Probably about 22,000 Lapps live in Norway, with some 15,000 or so of them in Finnmark. Their

Herding reindeer such as these is the traditional occupation of the Lapps.

traditional occupation is herding reindeer. Reindeer meat is used for food and the skins are made into clothing. Today, many Lapps are fishermen and farmers. They have their own newspaper and special radio programs in the Lapp language.

THE LANGUAGE

The basic Norwegian language is similar to English and German. There are currently two official tongues in the country. The standard is called *Bokmaal* ("book language"). The New Norwegian, based on local dialects, is called *Nynorsk*. The two are similar and easily understood by everyone and are gradually being combined into a single form called *Samnorsk*.

It wasn't an easy matter to agree on what the Norwegian language should be as changes occurred over the years. When foreign

governments controlled the country, the people picked up bits and pieces from all those other languages. The Norwegian language probably has been influenced most by Danish, because of the long-term occupation of Norway by Denmark.

After independence, there was a lot of discussion about what to choose as the official language of Norway. The dispute broke up more than one town hall meeting. In fact, in 1912, a prime minister quit his job because of the disagreement.

A language commission finally was set up in the late 1940s. It worked for almost ten years to come up with a common way of saying things. But it wasn't until the mid-1960s that the battle died out. By that time, many of the dialects no longer were being used because so many people had moved to the cities and lost their regional speech.

Norwegians enjoy a good argument and are skilled debaters. The fight over the language was a great national pastime as long as it lasted. The typical Norwegian is an individualist. Everyone in the country seems to have an opinion on almost any subject.

WORKING AND PLAYING

Norwegians are hard workers, although sometimes other Scandinavians chuckle at the way things get done in Norway. Perhaps it's because of the long winter nights, but the Norsk folk appear to be irregular in their work habits. The short summer season means that farmers have to squeeze a lot of field activity into a very tight time period. It's the same with fishermen, who spend around-the-clock hours on the sea while their catch is offshore. After this frantic rush, there is time to rest, tell stories, work on crafts, and get ready for the next season.

These potato farmers have to work very hard during Norway's very short growing season.

A dancing demonstration at a Norwegian folk museum

Norwegians play hard, as well. They enjoy festivals and holidays. Any excuse for a party will do. A rural Norwegian wedding traditionally has been one of the favorite forms of merrymaking. There aren't many of the old-time three- or four-day ceremonies anymore, however, except for dancing demonstrations in folklife programs. Today, most weddings are similar to those in other countries. Yet the old-time wedding involved everyone in the community, with plenty of handshaking, eating, and drinking.

Norwegian youngsters don't need a wedding in order to have a good time. Although much of the year Norway is cold and snowy, the weather doesn't keep children indoors. Norwegian children seem to thrive on the outdoors, regardless of the season.

Even in cold, snowy weather, Norwegians love the outdoors.

There are few nursery schools for small children in Norway, at least outside the major cities. So most of the little ones play on their own. The basically unspoiled nature of Norway, with the vast tracts of forestland, the expanse of mountains, and the beauty of the sea, are taken for granted. Snow is great for snowmen, sleds, toboggans, and skis, and there always is ice to skate on.

Summertime fun includes hiking, sailing, fishing, and camping. Norwegian children especially love going to camp. There are yachting camps where children learn all the techniques necessary for sailing, rowing, and lifesaving—important skills for these descendants of the Vikings.

At other summer camps, children learn about farm life. Some farms offer "bed and board" vacations for visiting young people. A few of these farms have *seters,* small log cabins, set out along pastures high in the mountains. Children can wake up in the morning and watch the cows right outside the window.

Other vacations offer lodgings in fishermen's homes in the Lofoten Islands or at Bjørnsund, near Molde. Children even like to stay in boathouses at Ferkingstad village on Kamoy Island. Pony-trekking excursions and hiking are also favorite summer activities.

Sometimes an entire class—students and teacher—heads for the mountains during the summer for special courses on plants and animals. And during this season, many American young people of Norwegian descent visit Camp Norway, a project of the Norwegian-American Cultural Institute, to learn about their heritage.

HOLIDAYS

Holidays are important in Norway. Put together some of the best holidays from around the world, with all their excitement, and you have an idea what Norway's *Syttende Mai* (Seventeenth of May) celebration is like. This day marks the signing of the Norwegian constitution in 1814 at Eidsvoll.

Hurrahs, bands, flags, parades, and dinners mark the day. Children march through the streets of every town, cheering and applauding their country. There are dances, films, sports, and other activities on into the evening.

The midsummer festival of St. Hans (or John), on June 24, is still celebrated in Norway much as it has been for hundreds of years. Originally, this feast was held in honor of the sun.

Crowds line the street as a parade marches down Karl Johans Gate in Oslo on Norway's national holiday, Syttende Mai, *in celebration of the signing of the constitution.*

Supposedly, the gates of the upper and lower worlds were opened at midsummer. Supernatural beings walked the earth and trolls and evil creatures threatened human beings, who protected themselves with huge bonfires

This tradition changed under Christianity. The festival was given a new meaning, this time in honor of St. John the Baptist. But some of the old ways still persist. Bonfires still are lighted on Midsummer Eve. Houses are decorated with birch boughs, symbolizing the new life that marks springtime and early summer.

July 29 is named in honor of St. Olav, the patron saint of Norway. The day commemorates the death of Olav Haraldson at the battle of Stiklestad near Trondheim in the year 1030. In Oslo there are religious observances, fireworks, and games.

Every year, the battle in which Olav died is reenacted. King Olav was supposed to have been a wise and just ruler, but he didn't actually exhibit many saintly characteristics while he was alive. Of course, it must have been difficult for him to be saintly while his throne was being besieged from all sides. Olav was made a saint after many miracles were reported by people who visited his grave site.

St. Olav became more prominent after the Reformation and until the time of independence. Norwegians were looking for national heroes. Olav became the symbol of everything good about Norway. When Prince Carl of Denmark was elected king of Norway in 1905, he changed the name of his two-year-old son Alexander to Olav, after the kingly saint. That popular decision helped ease the move into his adopted country. As you remember, Carl chose the old Norwegian name of Haakon, which was a double bonus in the eyes of the people.

Christmas is the favorite holiday of Norwegians.

Christmas is perhaps the favorite holiday in Norway. In the big cities, there is the same Yule rush as there is all over the Christian world. But an old saying in Norway is that Christmas lasts until Easter because nobody wants to end the festivities.

Norway's forests contribute to the festive air. Lighted Christmas trees are used on all public buildings. Trees are shipped to other European nations as gifts. On Norwegian ships, trees are tied to the masts and cooks plan huge on-board dinners.

A special Christmas beer, called the *juleol*, is brewed and many pork dishes are prepared. It's traditional to have at least seven varieties of cookies in each home, along with the *julekake*, a sweet bread filled with raisins and fruits. Rice porridge is a favorite with young people at Christmas dinner, especially since it is served with a single almond mixed into its feathery texture. The lucky finder receives a gift.

In the country, a bowl of porridge is always taken out to the barn for the resident *nisse*, the little elf who keeps a friendly watch over the farm animals. According to legend, if the bowl is empty in the morning, the farm will have good luck. If the bowl is untouched, then there's trouble ahead. Even the birds get a Christmas treat: the *julenek*, a sheaf of oats mounted on a pole, is set up in the yard.

Presents are opened on Christmas Eve, after the ritual known as "walking around the Christmas tree." The family members join hands and sing carols as they circle the brightly decorated tree.

Celebrations and parties are held all through the Christmas season, which usually lasts about twenty days, until the feast of St. Canute.

Another important holiday for Norwegians is United Nations Day, celebrated on October 24. Norway was a charter member of that world body. A Norwegian—Trygve Lie—was its first secretary-general.

RELIGION: CHURCH AND STATE

As we have seen, many of the important Norwegian holidays are religious in character. Religion is very important to the people of this country. Under the constitution, the Evangelical Lutheran

Church is the established church of Norway. The king is ordered to defend and maintain the church. Since Lutheranism is a state religion, the bishops and most of the pastors are appointed by the king, who is the "chief bishop." The state pays clergymen's salaries and churches are built with government funds. While almost 88 percent of the people belong to the Lutheran church, freedom of religion is encouraged.

It wasn't always that way, however. The old Norse religion was bloody, with the sacrifice of animals and slaves an important part of it. Many of the slaves probably were Christian, captured on raids to the south. No doubt they were able to spread Christianity throughout Norway. Eventually, even the kings were baptized. Norway was a Roman Catholic country for about five hundred years, a time when many churches were built. Many of them were the famous stave (wooden) churches with their high ceilings and ornate wood carvings.

It was several generations before Catholicism lost its hold on the people. In 1537 the Reformation washed over Norway. By the 1700s, the Lutheran religion was well established. As Norwegian sailors visited around the globe, however, they brought back other religions, such as Baptist, Methodist, and Adventist.

During World War II, the churchmen and churchwomen of Norway were very brave and often spoke out against the occupying Nazi forces. Many priests, bishops, ministers, and other religious leaders were imprisoned or put to death. That terrible time, when all religions suffered together, proved to Norwegians that they could work for a common goal regardless of how they worshipped.

The Lapps had a very interesting religion, although many of them now are Christian. Their ancient beliefs centered around the

The Arctic Cathedral at Tromsø

forces of nature and the worship of the sun, moon, thunder, and wind. The bear also held a prominent position for the Lapps and was considered half-human and half-divine. The *shaman,* or Lapp "priest," was the go-between for men and the spirit world. Many of the Lapps have been influenced by the Swedish clergyman Laestadius, who was active throughout Scandinavia about a hundred years ago.

Norwegian missionaries have been active in spreading their message around the world. As early as the 1700s, they were traveling to numerous countries to establish churches, schools, hospitals, and colleges, as well as to preach. The majority of Norwegian missionaries now work in Africa.

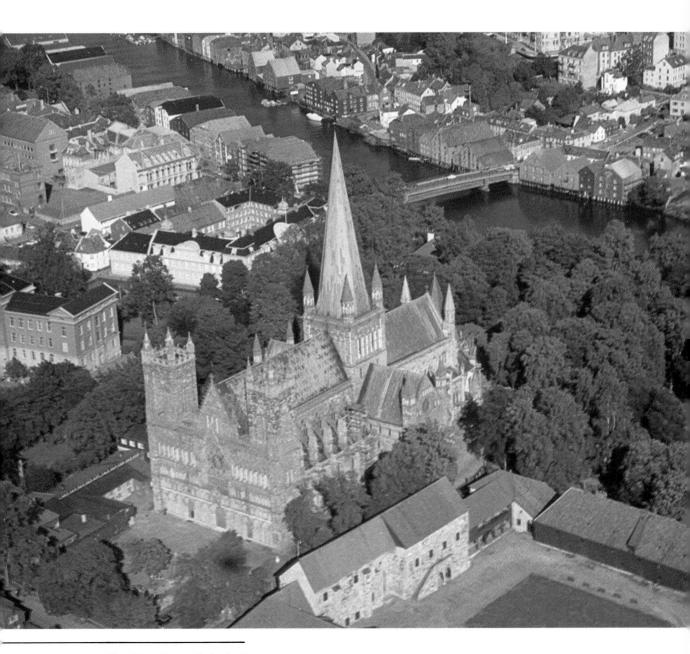

The Trondheim Cathedral

Most of Norway's food specialties come from the sea.

FOOD

Eating is a favorite pastime of Norwegians, with such delicacies as herring, goat cheese, and *lutefisk* (lye fish) topping the menu. The latter is a mushy mixture of skinned, dried cod and salt. A true Norwegian will swear that there is nothing better on the table, especially when it is served with boiled potatoes. That's a fact that is argued by non-lutefisk lovers who dislike its odor. Another smelly gourmet treat is *gammelost* (old cheese), which is somewhat greenish-brown.

A smorgasbord of Norwegian delicacies

Most of the nation's food specialties come from the sea. That's not surprising, since Norway has some 15,000 miles (about 24,000 kilometers) of coastline. But everything doesn't taste of the sea. Youngsters love *rommegrot,* a porridge made with thick, fresh cream and flour. It is boiled and thickened, then sprinkled with cinnamon and sugar.

Adults like the fiery taste of *akevitt,* a very strong liquor made from caraway seeds and potatoes. This national beverage is drunk at parties, while toasts are made all around. The word *skoal* is used at these happy times. It can mean either "to your health" or "good luck on that drink, don't burn out your pipes!"

Some other Norwegian dishes are *farikal* (mutton and cabbage), *fiskekaker* (codfish cakes), *lefse* (potato pancakes), *spekeskinke* (sweetened and smoked ham), *gravlaks* (smoked salmon), and a smorgasbord of similar culinary delights.

Today's Norwegians are a product of the past, tempered by a look toward the future. They are a wonderful mix of personality shaped and directed by generations of fine tradition. This shows up in their customs, religion, foods, holidays, and recreation. No wonder Norwegians are proud!

These hikers have a breathtaking view from one of Norway's many flat-topped mountains.

Chapter 3

NATURE'S ROCK-TOSSED PLAYGROUND

The term Norway (*Norge* in Norwegian) comes from the Viking word *Nordvegr,* meaning the "way to the North." It referred to the Viking route along the coast. Norway is a land of surprises, where mountain ranges tumble into the raging sea, where glaciers grind slowly down from the heights, where deep lakes and high plateaus merge. Less than 4 percent of the land can be farmed. Thus, many Norwegians must turn to the sea in order to live.

Geographically, the Norwegians have turned generally westward, toward the ocean. It was easier to venture in that direction, rather than battle a rough way eastward over the soaring cliffs of the interior. Some of the mountains are part of what is called the Jotunheimen range in south-central Norway. These are the highest mountains in Europe north of the Alps. A great number of Norway's mountains are not soaring peaks but are flat at the top. Anyone who does manage to struggle up them can hike around fairly easily.

Along the west coast are the famous fjords, those deep inlets into the mountains that are perfect subjects for beautiful postcards. Thousands of islands dot the ocean just offshore. They

*The warm water of the North Atlantic Current
helps keep Norway's harbors from freezing over.*

help protect the coast by breaking up the surf and the storms that
sweep across the North Atlantic. Strangely, Norway's harbors
seldom freeze over, despite her cold winters and the fact that the
Arctic Circle cuts across her northernmost territory. The warm
water of the North Atlantic Current flows north along the coast
and keeps ice from forming. Some of the best farming is in this
region because of the sheltered conditions along the sea. Even the
people in Hammerfest, the northernmost town in the world,
benefit somewhat from that flow.

Norway has an abundance of waterfalls and glaciers. All are
prime tourist attractions.

This waterfall near Foss is one of the hundreds that can be found in Norway.

The country is 1,100 miles long (1,770 kilometers) and varies in width from 4 to 280 miles (6.4 to 451 kilometers). About half of Norway is north of the Arctic Circle. In the Arctic, Norway has jurisdiction over Svalbard (Spitzbergen), Jan Mayen, and Bear islands. Norway even has some possessions at the opposite end of the world. Her Antarctic territories include Peter I and Bouvet islands, as well as the portion of the Antarctic continent called Queen Maud's Land.

On the landward side, more than 1,000 miles (1,609 kilometers) of Norway's frontier borders with Sweden. The remainder separates Norway from Finland and the former Soviet Union.

OSLO, CITY OF MUSEUMS

Most of the population lives near Oslo, where boating and bathing are popular. The sheltered coast, protected by numerous islands, is rich in recreational opportunities. This city at the head of Oslo Fjord has a strange mixture of heavy traffic and quiet parks. Very little of the city is old, even though it was founded hundreds of years ago. Terrible fires have swept through Olso. One of the worst, in 1624, nearly wiped the city from the map. But the Oslo residents came back to the rubble and rebuilt their homes. There was another bad fire in 1858.

Some travelers have said that Oslo's buildings look conservative and dull. But there is a solid, strong look about Norway's capital.

It is a city of museums. The Oslo Ship Museum houses numerous artifacts from the Viking age, as well as burial ships dug from the Norwegian clay years ago. Another fine museum honors the painter Edvard Munch. He left about twenty thousand of his works to the city of Oslo. The Oslo Historical Museum has some fascinating displays of Stone Age and Middle Age artifacts, especially carved figures from stave churches. The Kon-Tiki Museum is home to Thor Heyerdahl's famous raft, the *Kon-Tiki*, on which the Norwegian explorer drifted westward across the Pacific Ocean from Peru in 1947. He wanted to show that ancient mariners could have done the same thing. There are many other fine buildings housing such artifacts.

The oldest part of Oslo has yielded some rich treasures for archaeologists. They have unearthed the foundations of many buildings. One of these is the church in which several medieval kings were crowned. Nearby are the remains of an old fort that once was the bishop's palace.

This Viking warship, built about A.D. 900, is on exhibit at the Oslo Ship Museum.

Oslo residents shop for
fresh flowers and vegetables
at the open market called
the Stortorget (above).
The main government buildings
of Norway, including
parliament (the Storting),
are located in Oslo. The
picture at left shows
the opening of parliament.

Oslo

The Radhus (Oslo City Hall)

The harbor at Oslo

Panoramic view of Oslo, at the head of Oslo Fjord

Oslo is a haven for statues. Almost everywhere there are full-size and half-size statues, miniatures, and busts of famous and not-so-famous people. Not all of them are Norwegian. There is one statue of President Franklin D. Roosevelt of the United States, who praised Norway's bravery during World War II.

The main street in Oslo is Karl Johans Gate, named after the Swedish King Carl XIV, who became king of Norway in 1818. Along this street are most of the main government buildings of the country, including the Storting. Beyond that structure is an open market called the Stortorget where Oslo residents can buy fresh flowers and vegetables.

One of the best views of the city is from the Holmenkollen ski jump. There is an observation platform at the top of the jump. It is scary to peer over the rim of the jump and see what a skier sees when taking off. Near the structure is a ski museum that traces the history of this sport back at least two thousand years.

As a border district, the area around Oslo was often a battleground. Because of this, the region is rich in history. The many large manor houses are reminders of the days of Danish occupation.

The eastern valleys of Norway, to the north of Oslo, are fertile farming areas. They also are carpeted with forests. This is Norway's prime timber country and the lakes that dot the woodlands are great for holiday getaways.

Norway's longest river, the Glåma, edges through the district to empty into Oslo Fjord. Logs are floated downstream, on an easy route to the sawmills. Many of Norway's stories about trolls and giants come from this region. It is easy to see why. A constant whispering of wind-tickled pine trees drifts through a rugged landscape where only giants could walk easily.

Hallingdal Valley in the east of Norway

Two of the prettiest valleys, the Gudbrandsdal and Valdres systems, are popular tourist destinations. The Numedal and Hallingdal valleys are typically forest draped and are pocked with numerous small lakes. There are many picturesque farmhouses and stave churches in this district.

TELEMARK AND SORLANDET

The Telemark and Sorlandet regions have both coastal areas and great mountains. Telemark has some of the best skiing in the world, with its sky-grabbing cliffs and deep gorges. It also has had a grim history, especially during World War II. In one of its hidden valleys, Norwegian saboteurs blew up a plant used by the Nazis to produce material for atom-bomb experiments. Sorlandet, which means "The South Land," has enough coastal villages and harbors to delight any sailing fan. Mandal, at the tip of the land here, is the southernmost town in the nation.

Some of Norway's famous folk characters came from this

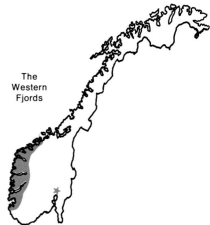

The Western Fjords

Geiranger Fjord, one of the western fjords

district. Among them were bands of cutthroats and tough characters who used to waylay travelers.

THE WESTERN FJORDS

The western fjords probably present the image of what most of us think of as Norway. The area reaches from Stavanger in the south to Kristiansund in the north. Many of the fjords are only a few hundred yards wide, with steep cliffs rising on each side. Others are very wide and easily entered by large ships. Some of the most beautiful waterfalls in Norway tumble over the cliffs and sparkle from rock to rock. Sometimes tiny farmhouses can be seen tucked into the mountains high above the water. The many orchards in this district are very lovely when the trees are in bloom. But the savagery of the ocean is ever present here, especially in the northern portion of the fjord country. Guidebooks warn of inlets where the sea pounds at the rocks and smashes ships piloted by careless sailors.

The famous Bergen fish market is on the harbor.

BERGEN, A MAGIC CITY

The "capital" of the western district is Bergen, an important commercial center for generations. The hub of the city is its harbor, and the fish market is famous. Bergen is accurately called a magic city because of the beauty of the surrounding countryside and the grace and charm of the town. The older parts of Bergen are great for walking tours, although much of central Bergen was destroyed by fires over the years. Therefore, it is fairly new in appearance. It is one of the oldest cities in Norway, having been founded in 1070 by Olav the Peaceful. But even before that, the Vikings used the harbor as a starting point for expeditions. Many Norwegian emigrants in the nineteenth century left from the Bergen harbor, seeking a new life overseas.

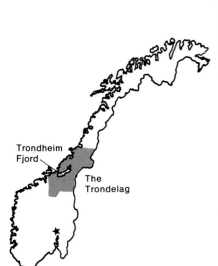

Trondheim Fjord

The Trondelag

The Old Bergen Museum is one of the city's many museums.

The Hanseatic League, the group of European cities that controlled much of the Norwegian trade for years in the Middle Ages, was very strong in Bergen.

Bergen is famous for its rainfall, and everyone carries an umbrella even when the sun is shining. A cloudburst can occur at any time. But the rains usually don't last very long and they give a fresh, sparkling look to everything.

The city is full of museums, ranging from the Municipal Art Museum to an Agricultural Museum and a Leprosy Museum. (Armauer Hansen of Bergen discovered the cause of that terrible sickness, also called Hansen's disease, in the 1870s and worked to find a cure.)

THE TRONDELAG

In the middle of Norway a fertile farming area lies on either side of the Trondheim Fjord. This district, called the Trondelag, contains mountains, valleys, and flat countryside. Many Vikings set out on explorations and raids from here. The Trondelag is the hub of Norway, linking the north and south with traditions as well as geography.

This Lapp in Finnmark is herding reindeer with a snow scooter.

THE NORTH AND FINNMARK

Northern Norway is an entirely different world—one of snowy landscapes and harsh mountain ridges. But it isn't a year-round frosty countryside. No other area in the world this far above the Arctic Circle is as warm. It can be called the Land of the Strawberries because of the climate, tempered as it is by the North Atlantic Current. A lot of that delicious fruit is grown here.

Finnmark, however—the extreme northland—is a vast plateau used mostly as pastureland for reindeer. From May to September there is almost constant daylight. But during the remainder of the year, both days and nights are almost entirely shaded in the dusk of evening. Much of this land was covered by ice only about ten thousand years ago, a very short time in the history of the world.

Despite the rugged conditions, people probably have lived here since the last retreating ice melted. But now most of the people in Finnmark are said to live within walking distance of the ocean. At least that is where the only important towns are located. A good highway links the settlements, ferryboats ply the coastline, and planes fly into the interior.

Longyearbyen

SVALBARD (Spitzbergen)

Oslo

Norway is famous as the Land of the Midnight Sun.

THE LAND OF THE MIDNIGHT SUN

The climate of Norway is relatively mild considering its northern location. Winter runs from November to March. The coldest spots are found in some inland valleys, in the mountain districts of south-central Norway, and on the Finnmark plateau.

During part of the summer, the midnight sun can be seen. From midnight to midnight, the sun never sinks below the horizon. At the town of Longyearbyen, in Svalbard, the midnight sun lasts from April 21 to August 8. The best times to experience the midnight sun are during the first or last weeks of the summer season. Then the sun sets and rises again within an hour.

The coastal regions of Norway have the most rain. Inland it's a different story, with some places getting barely four inches (about ten centimeters) of rain a year. The far northern stretches of Finnmark get the most snow, which hugs the ground until early summer. Sometimes the snow towers over both sides of a road after plows push their way through. In very bad winter weather, traffic is escorted across the mountains in long convoys. They are led by snowplows and followed by a road crew that takes care of stragglers and drivers who get stuck in the drifts. Often the blizzards are so bad that travelers have to stay inside one of the mountain tunnels. But special heating rooms have been built there so motorists can wait in comfort.

In the spring, melting snow often causes problems. The water rushes over the roads and sometimes even washes away the surface gravel. This is occasionally a problem on the E6 highway, the longest continuous main road in Norway.

GETTING AROUND

The E6 crosses the Arctic Circle on the Saltfjell plateau. In this area the weather can become very bad very quickly. Because it is the only permanent road connection between northern and southern Norway, the highway is kept open even during the worst storms. Many bridges are being constructed across the fjords, so motorists don't have to make zigzag trips all along the coastline. Some of the bridges have replaced ferryboats, but several vessels still make fun-filled trips across the sparkling, deep-blue waters.

Traffic in Norway moves on the right side of the road, as it does in the United States. But in Norway, it is often easier to get around

These passengers are enjoying a ferryboat trip across a Norwegian fjord.

by train. Bus service is also quick and efficient, as is coastal passenger-service by small boat. Travelers can be transported by large cruise ships, ferryboats, small boats called *skerries,* and local steamers. In fact, the oldest paddle-wheel ship still working in the world chugs between Eidsvoll and Lillehammer from early June to mid-August. The *Skibladner,* built in 1856, works as well as it did when it was launched.

Finding a room to stay in Norway is no problem. There are more than four hundred hotels in the country, including popular mountain resorts called the *hoyjellshotell.* In addition to these fancy places, farm guesthouses, lodges, hostels, and chalets are open for travelers and vacationers.

These sheep are grazing
in the beautiful
Hallingdal region (left).

Thousands of birds nest
in this cliff at the edge of
the water (below left).

Polar bears (below right)
live in the Arctic regions
in the far north.

ANIMAL LIFE

The traveler in Norway is often treated to fascinating sights of the country's animal life, from reindeer to smaller creatures. The lemming is a tiny rodent, with yellow and black or gray fur. It is rarely seen by anyone but the most patient observer. The lemming seldom comes out of its nest, except at night to munch on local vegetation. The average female lemming has three to four litters of babies a year, with as many as ten little ones in each batch. Of course, that soon makes for overcrowding.

The lemmings then migrate, eating almost anything in their way. Millions of lemmings patter across the countryside, for some reason always heading toward the ocean. When they come to the edge of the seaside cliffs, they can't stop their forward rush and are pushed over by the weight of the bodies behind them. The few lemmings that are left—those lucky fellows from the rear ranks—then get back to the business of eating, sleeping, and making more little lemmings so the process can start all over.

Norway has the usual collection of domestic animals: cows, goats, sheep, pigs, horses, chickens, and so on. Its list of wild creatures includes the wolf, lynx, otter, and fox, with even an occasional bear in the far north. Millions of seabirds make their nests along the northern and western coasts of Norway. Many are migratory. Before the winter season sets in, they leave for warmer Mediterranean and African climates. Ducks, grouse, puffins, and warblers are only a few of the birds that live in Norway. Insects are plentiful, and the mosquito is especially annoying in the forests and swamps during the summer months.

Fish are very important to the life-style of Norwegians. Familiar sights all along the coastline are the drying racks where cod is

Codfish drying racks such as this one at Hammerfest are familiar sights all along the coastline of Norway.

cured for several weeks before being shipped out. The warm Atlantic mixing with colder northern waters makes a fine spawning ground for all sorts of saltwater fish. Trout and salmon fill the lakes and rivers. Whales and seals also can be found offshore.

PLANT LIFE

Norway has about two thousand varieties of plants. The most noticeable, of course, are the spruce and pine trees in the huge tracts of forest land that seem to cover almost the entire countryside. Vegetation is thickest in the southern part of Norway. The mountain plateaus, however, are rich with heather, wild flowers, and grass.

The Briksdal Glacier (above left) is a prime tourist attraction.
Wild flowers carpet much of the land throughout Norway (above right).
Norwegians appreciate the beauty that surrounds them and work hard to make
sure that areas like these remain unspoiled for future generations.

Norwegians are very conscious of the importance of
environmental protection. After long years of study, the country
established a Ministry of Environment in 1972. Ways had to be
found to take care of the land the Norwegians had long enjoyed.
The goal is to guard nature's ability to reproduce, as well as to
ensure future growth.

A number of national parks and nature reserves have been set
up. There also are about twenty protected landscape areas, as well
as wild-animal preserves and bird sanctuaries.

Norwegians appreciate and love their closeness with the
outdoors. They are determined to keep their country in the
unspoiled state in which they received it from their ancestors.

Skiing in a rugged country

Chapter 4

SPORTING IN A RUGGED COUNTRY

There is hardly an excuse for Norwegians not to enjoy their outdoors. The spread of mountain, ocean, lake, river, and tundra presents marvelous recreational opportunities. Almost everyone heads for the quiet countryside at any leisure moment. Skiing, because of the nature of the land, is the most popular sport in the country. Norwegians always can be sure of getting around in the wintertime, since skiing has practical uses as well.

Skiers were zooming over Norway 2,500 years ago. In Norse mythology, Ull was the ski god and Skade was the ski goddess. They may have looked like some of today's handsome men and beautiful women who hotdog across the ridges. In the days of the Norsemen, skiing was considered the sport of kings.

There's a wonderful story about how two of the king's fastest skiers saved the life of his son, Haakon Haakonson, during the civil war of 1206. The men smuggled the two-year-old boy out of war-torn territory from Gudbrandsdal to Osterdal. That trip over the mountains is remembered each winter with a marathon ski race between Lillehammer and Rena. The skiers follow the same route used by the "Birch Legs," as the two skiing heroes were nicknamed.

Now skiing has become everyman's sport. Huge crowds gather at Holmenkollen ski-jumping hill outside Oslo to watch skiers hurl down the slope at what seems to be a million miles an hour.

The Norwegian military held ski competitions as far back as 1767. The first civilian ski race took place in 1843. It wasn't long before teams and clubs were organized. At least four thousand Norwegians were taking part in ski events by the 1880s. Another fifty thousand or so were using skis to get back and forth to work.

During the emigration years, the Norwegians carried their love of skiing with them. They were surprised to discover that few people in foreign lands knew about it. That ignorance didn't last long once the Norwegians started showing their skills. Soon skiing was popular all around the world.

While the Norwegians may have exported skiing, the British exported mountain climbing. This sport is becoming very popular with the Norsk set. On bright days, people crawl across sheer ledges high overhead, tied together only by thin strands of rope. It takes a special kind of courage to tackle that sort of athletic fun. Soccer is a popular sport, as it is throughout the world, and gymnastics is close behind. Golf and tennis are gaining more fans as well. Hardly anyone jogs as much as Americans do. Norwegians prefer to hike, bicycle, or swim to stay in shape.

More than a million Norwegians are enrolled in sports clubs. These have been broken down into regional groupings. There is even a special sailors league, called the *sjomannsidretten,* or "Seaman's Sports." Crews pit their skills in several different sports against the crews of other ships.

Schools up to the university level have compulsory physical education, but sports are not organized on a school basis as they are in the United States. Most sports are run by clubs. Many

Queen Sonja assists skiers in a sports program for the handicapped.

businesses sponsor athletic teams in a number of sports. By the 1980s, about four thousand such teams were competing on many levels.

Programs for the handicapped also are very important in Norway. Participation in sports helps keep the handicapped healthy and in touch with the outside world. There are special sports centers and sports clubs especially for the handicapped.

Olympic figure-skating champion Sonja Henie

The reason for all this activity is the Norwegian belief that a healthy body helps make a healthy mind and soul. There is a growing concern that too much emphasis has been placed on winning in a sport. But up to now, most Norwegians care less about winning than having a good time and some exercise. Which is not to say Norwegians aren't competitive. They do very well in Olympic events and other competitions.

For instance, the famous woman figure skater, Sonja Henie, was born in Oslo. She began figure skating when she was eight years old. Two years later, she captured the first of six consecutive Norwegian skating championships. She then went on to win the European figure-skating championships ten years in a row. Sonja won Olympic figure-skating gold medals in 1928, 1932, and 1936. After those victories, she moved to the United States where she starred in Hollywood movies and produced her own ice show. Sonja Henie died in 1969 at the age of fifty-six.

Norwegians have no professional sports or teams. These independent folk prefer their amateur status.

The Norwegians get paid holidays and a large amount of vacation time. They begin work early and return home early. This leaves a lot of time to enjoy a weekend trip to the mountains or the ocean or a late-afternoon jaunt out of town.

Chapter 5

LAND OF CARING

Norway is ruled by King Harald V. He succeeded on the death
of his father, King Olav V on January 21, 1991. King Olav V was a
king who enjoyed being with his people. Every May 17 — Norway's
Independence Day — the king and royal family would stand for
hours on the palace balcony in Oslo. Thousands of schoolchildren
paraded past to shout their hellos up to him as he waved back.

Even on the street, countrymen greeted the king simply by
saying, "Hi, Your Majesty." Every year Olav received hundreds of
people in special palace audiences giving them opportunity to
speak "officially" to their monarch. King Harald V continues
these traditions.

THE ROYAL FAMILY

Norway is a country that takes its monarchy seriously, but not
too seriously. Olav didn't care for gilded carriages or thrones. He
often said that he preferred sailing, hiking, and skiing to the
trappings of royalty. Olav became king in September 1957 after
being crown prince for more than fifty years. He was born in
England on July 2, 1903. His Danish father came to rule

Norway when the country hadn't had its own king for a long time.

King Olav's ancestors were kings and queens of Denmark, Sweden, and Great Britain. He could trace his history back thirty-four generations to King Harald Fair Hair, who united Norway in A.D. 872.

When Olav's wife, the Swedish Princess Martha, died in 1954, three years before he became king, Olav never remarried. So since the death of Olav's mother, Queen Maud, in 1938, no woman had shared the throne.

Olav had two daughters, the Princesses Ragnhild and Astrid, who have no claims on the throne. Both are married to Norwegian businessmen. Ragnhild and her husband, Erling Lorentzen, who is director of a shipping firm, live with their three children in Rio de Janeiro, Brazil. Astrid and her husband, Johan Martin Ferner, live in a house on the outskirts of Oslo with their four children.

When Crown Prince Harald, Olav's only son and heir to the throne, decided to marry a commoner, it caused some protests. Some had to be convinced that it was proper for their next ruler not to marry nobility. But Harald's wife, Sonja, won over the hearts of the people. Her father-in-law, King Olav, designated her a crown princess. Sonja's Cinderella story reached a happy ending when she and Harald were married on August 29, 1968, in Oslo Cathedral. Four other kings, a grand duke, and three presidents attended the ceremony. Princess Sonja, now Queen Sonja, continues to win with her people as she assists social programs.

The crown prince and princess, now the king and queen, had a daughter, Princess Martha Louise born on September 22, 1971, and a son, Crown Prince Haakon Magnus born July 20, 1973. The monrachy is hereditary and as of 1990 the crown passes on to either a male or female heir.

Norway's royal family waves from the palace balcony on Constitution Day (Syttende Mai).

THE PEOPLE'S KING

A king's job in Norway is very important, although it is mostly ceremonial. "All for Norway" was Olav's motto, just as it was his father's, and is now Harald's. As has been customary in Norway, neither Olav nor Harald were crowned king, as there is no coronation ceremony. There was a simple blessing ceremony performed at Nidaros Cathedral.

In a modern constitutional monarchy like Norway, the king has no real power. He is the symbol of the nation's unity and independence. The king exercises what power he does have through the *Statsraad*, or council of state, which he appoints. Formally, the king decides the issues to be discussed by the council. However, all royal resolutions take effect only when countersigned by the prime minister or a senior member of the Statsraad. So actually, the council, along with the Storting, is the real authority in Norway.

Another important duty for the king is commanding the Norwegian armed forces, but unlike his work with the Statsraad, the king doesn't need a cosigner for military decisions.

King Olav spent a lot of time visiting with his countrymen and traveling to other nations as an official representative of Norway. Other members of the royal family also acted as special ambassadors. For instance, Crown Prince Harald visited Tokyo in 1964 as a member of the Norwegian Olympic sailing team.

Wherever he stopped, King Olav enjoyed meeting people and talking with them. When the royal yacht docked, it was cause for celebration. Local children and townspeople greeted him with flowers and singing. Harald became accustomed to the ceremony of the monarchy early on.

Like his father before him, Harald is a firm believer in the Norwegian constitution. That document provides for a limited monarchy and separation of powers. This means that the king has certain responsibilities, as does the Storting. According to the constitution, the king serves as head of state, although he can still influence decision making because he is independent of any political party. Essentially, the monarch's power is primarily symbolic.

The Parliament has the greatest power, with all members of the entire government being responsible to the Storting. Executive power is under the control of the cabinet and prime minister. Legislative and money-raising powers rest with the Storting. The courts are part of the judicial system.

A SYMBOL OF FREEDOM

To Norwegians, the constitution is more than a listing of laws on paper. It is their declaration of independence and their symbol of freedom. That's why May 17 is celebrated with such excitement.

Basically, the constitution gave the Norwegians the right and authority to choose a type of government. They chose the independent monarchial system. The constitution also put into force the separation of powers. It stressed human rights and included a number of amendments similar to the Bill of Rights in the United States Constitution. Of course, as times changed, more amendments were added. But basically, the Norwegians have been very cautious about changing anything. They like the document as it is and are proud of everything it stands for.

Under the Norwegian system of government, the parliament, or Storting, is made up of 165 seats, with members from the 6 major political parties. Norway is divided into 19 counties consisting of 448 municipalities. Oslo, the capital, is a county by itself.

Political decisions in both counties and municipalities are made by elected officials. Local elections are held every four years, midway between parliamentary elections. Everyone busily campaigns for his or her candidate. It is considered a great honor to be elected to any governmental post in Norway. All posts carry a great deal of responsibility. Everyone over eighteen may vote. And every citizen of voting age is qualified to be elected to the Storting.

The Storting has established an *ombudsman* system. Any citizen with a complaint that can't be handled in the courts may discuss it with the proper authorities. This is a tradition handed down over the generations. A Norwegian with a problem likes to be able to talk it over with someone in authority.

CARING AND SHARING

Norway has had many difficulties throughout her history. Some were hard to solve, even through the combined efforts of the king, the Storting, and the people. Yet the country has been able to survive and grow strong.

One of the roughest times was immediately after World War II when it was necessary to rebuild the Norwegian economy, government, and social system. There were critical shortages of raw materials, food, and the conveniences of modern society. Under strict government planning, the country came alive again.

In politics, the Labor Party made great gains throughout most of the years after the war. Eventually, however, it lost control of the Storting. But with the aid of various socialist parties in the early 1980s, it was able to recapture its power. Today, the Norwegian government takes a middle-of-the-road course, with no extreme political divisions.

But the social philosophies and practices of the postwar years had a great influence on the current life-style of the average Norwegian. Welfare programs that had been started before the war were broadened and strengthened. There was a strong feeling that Norwegians had to stick together and share what they had. The public-sickness-assistance program was made compulsory for the entire country by 1957. In 1967, the National Insurance System brought together a number of aid packages. Old-age pensions, health insurance, unemployment insurance, and many similar policies were combined. The entire system is paid for by contributions from insured persons, employers, municipalities, and the national government.

Each community has a social-welfare board of several members. The board plans the general welfare program, provides information to people in need, and handles applications for assistance. It also can give grants, help find a nursing home, aid in finding a trade, and assist in countless other ways.

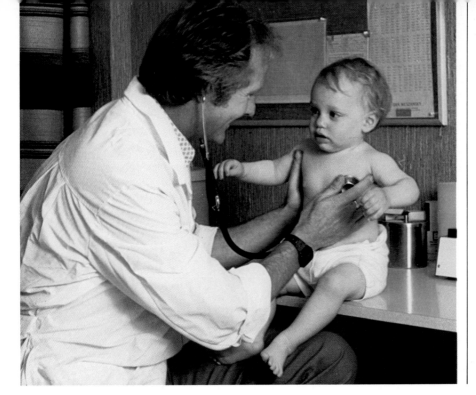

Young and old receive free health care in Norway. This baby is being examined at a local health station.

Local boards of health are responsible for health care. Since 1860, there has been a series of special health laws. Each of Norway's counties has a full-time public health office.

Under the national health-insurance plan, free hospital care is provided. Even funeral payments are included in the plan. A Norwegian may choose his own doctor and hospital. Everyone between the ages of six and eighteen may receive free dental care. Most of those over eighteen pay a fixed rate for dental care.

The Norwegians do admit that there are some problems in seeing that everyone gets equal care. There is a shortage of doctors and other medical workers in some of the outlying regions. The government is attempting to correct that.

Generally, Norwegians are satisfied with this "birth-to-death" arrangement and are working to make it even better. They feel that no one should be dependent on handouts or charity for his or her basic needs.

Norwegian women as well as men work at just about every career. These women have jobs at a fish-processing plant.

WORKERS AND WOMEN'S RIGHTS

The cooperative movement in Norway is very old, having started in the 1870s. It extends throughout the farming and fishing industries. This again demonstrates the willingness of the Norwegian to help a neighbor. The co-ops enable farmers to buy machinery and supplies at lower prices than would be possible from private companies.

There is little unemployment in Norway, even though a lot of the work is seasonal because of the weather. Workers are well protected under Norwegian law. The labor unrest of the Depression era is grimly remembered. Labor regulations aim to maintain safety standards, help with contracts, and assist businesses and workers in solving environmental problems.

The trade union movement is very strong in Norway. It is directed by the National Federation of Unions, which was started in 1899. In 1900, employers set up their own organization, the Norwegian Employers Confederation to help in bargaining.

Norwegian women as well as men have jobs outside the home. They are airline pilots, doctors, lawyers, and factory specialists. They work at just about every career, including that of homemaker. The idea of equality has grown stronger in Norway over the past twenty-five years, much as it has elsewhere in the world. The Norwegian Association for Women's Rights was founded in 1884. This organization, and others, have worked to get women voting rights, made sure that women could remain financially independent in marriage, and tackled a wide range of other causes. Norwegian women were given the right to vote in 1913, making Norway the first nation in the world to grant this privilege.

Famous Norwegian women in the field of women's rights include Camilla Collett and Aasta Hansteen. In the 1930s, Margaret Bonnevie led the movement to allow married women the right to work outside the home. It was due to their efforts, and to those of farsighted male colleagues, that an Equal Status Act was eventually passed by the Storting in 1978. This act officially guarantees women's rights in Norwegian society.

TEACHING AND LEARNING

Every Norwegian child must attend school for at least nine years. In 1739, a law required that each parish teach its youngsters how to read and write, figure problems, and understand religious teachings. Eventually, grammar schools were organized. Children could attend them on a regular basis. Those who could afford it sent their children to the major cities in Norway or elsewhere in Europe for more-advanced schooling. But soon Norwegian schools rivaled those of other countries.

These vocational-school students (above left) are learning to be cooks.
Kindergarten children (above right) are working with paints and clay.

Students usually start school when they are seven years old. The basic school system involves six years in a *barneskole* (lower primary school) and three in an *ungdomsskole* (upper primary school). Students usually attend for thirty-eight weeks of the year, going six days a week. Education is free, though university students must buy their own books.

After the primary schools, a student might then attend an institution that is equivalent to an American high school. This involves three years of special study. At the end of the course, a very difficult examination is given. The test results determine whether or not a student may attend a university.

There are also commercial schools, offering vocational and technical training. Norwegian students are now discovering that

The University of Trondheim (above) is one of four universities in Norway. The other three are located in Oslo, Bergen, and Tromsø.

the *folkehoyskoler,* the folk schools that were started in the nineteenth century, are exciting and interesting. They offer courses in arts and crafts, music, poetry, and other such subjects.

There are also several maritime schools in Norway, in keeping with the country's lively interest in the sea. They are of three main types: one for navigation, another for engineering, and a third for cooks and stewards. It's no wonder that the Norwegian merchant marine is one of the best, and that many of the finest cruise ships afloat are Norwegian.

Education is very important in Norway and students are encouraged to attend for as many years as possible. Teachers are held in high regard, as are those students who make it through to graduation.

Agriculture is one of the mainstays of the Norwegian economy. Most farms are small ones that are owned by the families who operate them.

Chapter 6

A NATION OF
ACHIEVERS

The Norwegians are industrious, imaginative, and forward looking. Generally, they enjoy a high standard of living.

The mainstays of the Norwegian economy have been agriculture, forestry, shipping, and fishing. From the 1980s into the 1990s, emphasis shifted to the service sector and oil-related and advanced industries. In 1993, Norway was the world's third largest exporter of petroleum and the sixth largest exporter of natural gas. Norway is a strong dairy-products exporter, with much pasture used for cows and goats.

AGRICULTURE

Wheat, oats, rye, and potatoes are the main crops. Fruit is grown in the Oslo area and throughout the fjord country. One interesting "crop" is Norwegian fur, primarily mink and blue fox. In the northland, reindeer are vital to the Lapp economy. Large herds roam the tundra, followed by herders and their families.

More than 85 percent of the farmland is operated by those who own the land. Many Norwegian farmers hold other jobs as well, working in factories or on fishing boats, for instance. The large wooden farmhouses that dot the countryside are snug and warm during the long winters.

Forestry is an important industry in Norway.

FORESTRY

The pulp and paper industry is very important to Norway. About 20 percent of the country is made up of forest land that can be used for a timber crop. Most of the trees are spruce, though there are pine and other species as well. The industry is helped by a number of factors. The many rivers and lakes make it easy for logs to be transported to mills and pulp factories, which are run by relatively inexpensive hydroelectric power. The ice-free ports are a bonus for shippers, as are the short distances to the main markets in Great Britain and on the European continent. The production of fine newspaper stock, magazine paper, and packaging-grade papers are Norwegian specialities. But the Norwegians are careful to guard the environment and reforest the land they've cleared.

Nusfjord (above), one of the countless fjords in Norway, is located in the Lofoten Islands.

FISHING

With a shoreline consisting of endless fjords and offshore islands, plus the warm waters of the North Atlantic Current, fishing is excellent in Norway. Cod, herring, and other fish spawn in the region.

The sport of inland fishing attracts fishermen to Norway from all over Europe.

Boats and gear used to require only a small amount of money. Over the past few years, however, modern technology has affected the fishing scene. Bigger and faster boats, electronic equipment, and many other improvements have changed fishing patterns. More and more, the fleets venture farther away from home, spending weeks at sea in large factory ships so they can bring in more fish.

Norway has long been a great fishing country, with a major portion of the catch being processed before it is sold. Much of it is salted, but quite a lot of the fish is filleted and frozen as well. Much of it is exported.

Inland fishing is not as profitable as the deep-sea activity, but it is important nonetheless. The sport of salmon fishing attracts fishermen to Norway from all over Europe and boosts the tourist trade. Trout abound in most rivers and lakes, but it takes a great deal of angling skill to land one of the huge Norwegian game fish. It can be done, though, and the prize is worth all the work.

Shipbuilding is a traditional occupation for many Norwegians. This is the shipyard at Haugesund.

The last major expedition was in the mid-1960s because of a scarcity of whales. Then Soviets and Japanese took over commercial whaling. By 1993 Norway resumed commercial whaling on certification that whale stock was no longer in danger of extinction. In 1994 Norway again opposed a ban on commercial whaling in the Antarctic. There is a whaling museum on Oslo Fjord.

SHIPPING

The Vikings once hauled cargo all along the Norwegian coast in wider, heavier ships than the karfi, the dragon ships, they used for war. All those long years of tradition have made the Norwegians

Oil found in the North Sea led to the development of a petrochemical industry in the early 1970s. This oil rig is being towed to the oil fields.

skilled sailors and boatmakers. In 1987 Norway established the Norwegian International Ship Register (NIS) to make it easier for ships to sail under the Norwegian flag. By 1990 Norwegian shipowners gained control of 10 percent of the world fleet.

The officers and masters and about three fourths of the seamen in the country's fleet are Norwegians. The merchant fleet is one of the largest in the world. Many Norwegian schools adopt a ship as a class project, sending letters and gifts to the crew at sea. Sailors often visit when they return to port.

ENERGY

While Norway has to import its gasoline, the dams and harnessed waterfalls in the country produce an abundance of electricity. Most of the electrical energy is used by factories, most notably by the growing aluminum-processing industry.

Other important energy sources are the oil and gas found at the end of the 1960s in the North Sea. Commercial exploitation was started in 1971. This has led to the development of a petrochemical industry in Norway. Because of the Norwegian

Most trains in Norway are electric.

concern for the environment, and the knowledge that its fishing industry depends on clean water, the drilling is closely watched.

Norway is in the happy position of exporting, or sending out, more goods than she has to import, or bring in. More exports means more money coming in for the goods sold. The country would like to keep that positive trend going.

TRANSPORTATION AND COMMUNICATION

Railways are very important in Norway—almost as important as the fleet of coastal vessels. Most trains are electric—massive cargo haulers so vital to getting up, down, and around the Norwegian mountains. The rest of the locomotives are diesel powered. The first railway in the country opened in 1854. It ran from Oslo to Eidsvoll. From then on, the rail industry was rather a piecemeal operation. Some of the difficulties were in construction.

Even though plows had cut a tunnel through the snow, these train tracks did not remain clear for long.

Tunnels had to be blasted out of the cliffs and snow shelters had to be built.

Airlines bring visitors to Norway from all parts of the world. The Scandinavian Airlines System (SAS), partially owned by the Norwegian government, is the main carrier into the country.

Short-range flights are handled by private companies or individuals. Skis are used on some of the planes during the winter and pontoons during the summer. So landing is a breeze almost anywhere at any time.

Since the Norwegians are avid readers, the publishing business is very strong. No one has to go very far to buy a paper. Everyone has a favorite magazine, newspaper, or book. The Norwegian press is very outspoken. Editors say exactly what is on their minds. Many political parties have their own papers and enjoy attacking the others' positions. The basic news columns, in true journalistic traditon, are generally quite fair.

Norway is a progressive country eager to ensure that all sectors of its society remain top-notch. Norwegians agree that it is the quality of life presented through the work and dedication of the people that will keep it that way.

Chapter 7

SOME FAMOUS NORWEGIANS

Norwegians have long made great contributions to the well-being of the world community. They have been active in many fields, from politics to exploration, from the arts to sports, from science to architecture. They are a dedicated people, with high ideals. They also seem to thrive on excitement and adventure.

THE NOBEL PRIZES

A number of prominent Norwegians have won Nobel Prizes in various fields. The prizes were set up by Alfred Nobel, the Swede who invented dynamite. They are very high honors and those who receive them are greatly respected.

Chemists Derek H.R. Barton, from England, and Norwegian Odd Hassel shared the Nobel Prize in chemistry in 1969. In that same year, Ragnar Frisch received a Nobel in economics. Other prizes are awarded in physics, medicine, literature, and peace. The physics, chemistry, and economics prizes are awarded by the Royal Academy of Science in Stockholm, Sweden. The prize for medicine is awarded by the Caroline Institute in Stockholm. The prize for literature is awarded by the Swedish Academy of Literature in Stockholm.

Nobel, in his 1895 will, stipulated that the Norwegian Storting appoint a committee to award the peace prize in his name. Nobel respected the Norwegians for their work in international law and felt that they would be highly qualified for this important job.

The committee studies the nominees and announces the winner in October each year. The prize-giving ceremony is held in Oslo on December 10, the anniversary of Nobel's death. There are festivities in both Stockholm, the capital of Sweden, and in Oslo.

This peace prize has been awarded more than sixty times. It has sometimes been shared by several people or institutions that have worked to help humanity. Two of the American winners have been George Catlett Marshall (1953), originator of the Marshall Plan that helped rebuild Europe after World War II, and civil-rights leader Reverend Martin Luther King, Jr. (1964).

Organizations that have won this famous award include the United Nations Children's Fund (UNICEF, 1965), the International Labor Organization (1969), and Amnesty International (1977).

The Norwegians take very seriously their role in naming the award winners and spend a great deal of time reviewing the fifty or so nominations.

Fridtjof Nansen, a Norwegian Arctic explorer, scientist, and humanitarian, received the Nobel Peace Prize in 1922 for his assistance to refugees and people without countries to call their own.

In 1921, Nansen was appointed League of Nations High Commissioner for Refugees, aiding people who had lost their homes in war or who had been prisoners. Among other things, he set up a passport for stateless persons, a special document that allowed them to cross borders without trouble.

Fridtjof Nansen and his ship, the Fram

Even before that fine work, Nansen was well known for his explorations. He made his first trip to the Arctic in 1882. In 1885, Nansen crossed Greenland on skis. His love for the polar regions led him to organize another expedition. He went farther into the frozen wilderness than anyone had ever gone before. His work provided valuable information to other explorers. His specially built ship, the *Fram,* is now on exhibit at the Maritime Museum near Oslo.

*Norwegian explorer Roald Amundsen (left)
was killed in 1929 attempting to rescue his
pilot, Umberto Nobile, who had crashed in a
separate incident. Thor Heyerdahl's balsa-wood
raft, the* Kon-Tiki *(below), is on exhibit
at the Kon-Tiki Museum in Oslo.*

MODERN EXPLORERS

The *Fram* also was used by another famous Norwegian adventurer, Roald Amundsen, the first man to reach the South Pole. He reached the pole on December 14, 1911, after a mad dash across the ice by dog sled and skis. He then turned his attention to air explorations, and in 1925 attempted to fly over the North Pole. But that trip was a failure. The next year, he and his pilot, Umberto Nobile, successfully made the journey in a dirigible called the *Norge.* The two saw previously unknown sections of the Arctic Ocean.

Thor Heyerdahl, yet another modern Viking explorer, wanted to prove that the first settlers of the Polynesian islands in the Pacific Ocean were from South America. So in 1947, he and several friends built a raft of balsa wood and drifted from Peru to the Tuamotu Islands. His adventures were described in the popular book *Kon-Tiki.*

In 1970, Heyerdahl sailed in a papyrus boat from Morocco to Barbados in the Caribbean Sea, trying to show that ancient mariners from the Mediterranean could have accomplished a similar feat. This was discussed in his book *The Ra Expeditions.*

Famous Norwegians in other fields who lent their skills and talents to making a better world include mathematician Niels Henrik Abel (1802-1829) and Kirsten Flagstad (1895-1962), one of the greatest singers of modern times, who later became head of the Norwegian State Opera. Well-known Norwegian-Americans range from politicians to newspaper editors, from chemists to poets. They seem to preserve the love of involvement, the spirit of discovery, and the drive for a better world that has characterized Norwegians through the centuries.

Chapter 8

FOLKTALES, MUSIC, ART, AND LITERATURE

Norway has as many folktales as there are trees in Rogaland. This surplus of stories must have something to do with the nature of the country. Its majestic open spaces, towering mountains, and spreading forests present a rich background for an imaginative people. It is easy to imagine stories of giants and trolls being told around some lonely campfire, with a breath of wind whispering through the spruce branches as if something out there were watching. Then there are the sagas, legends of bigger-than-life men battling fantastic beasts or fierce warriors from another world. Those Viking stories were told and retold by many generations of skalds. Each skald, of course, added a bit more color and drama to heighten the fun of listening.

The music of Norway can be as brooding as a winter landscape at Narvik, as lively as the sound of a waterfall, or as deep and powerful as the seas off the coasts. Norwegian composers have played harmonics with their world, and have created a vibrancy unmatched anywhere else. Painters, sculptors, and craftspeople of all kinds also have drawn on Norway itself as their ultimate inspiration.

This hapless gnome is in the temporary clutches of a wicked, but not very clever, troll.

TROLL TALES, FOLKTALES, AND SAGAS

Trolls are those gruesome folktale critters who spent their time making life miserable for unwary human beings and captured gnomes. The nisse, or barn elf, was usually a pleasant sort around the farm. But the troll was incredibly grumpy.

According to the stories, these unhappy creatures lived throughout Scandinavia. But evil as they may have been, trolls often met their match in creatures far more clever.

The story of the three Billy Goats Gruff is a good example. The goats had to cross a bridge over a stream. Under the bridge, the tale goes, lived a troll "with eyes as big as saucers and a nose as long as a poker." The two smaller goats made their way across safely by urging the hungry troll to wait for their bigger brother, who would make a better supper. The greedy troll did exactly that, grabbing for the biggest goat when he ambled across the bridge. But the goat promptly knocked the troll into the water. He then joined his brothers on the far side of the bridge.

Trolls were never known for their cleverness. They usually

prowled around at night because they couldn't stand the light of day. After getting into all kinds of trouble, they would scurry back to their cave homes before the sun came up. The sun could turn them into stones if they weren't careful.

At night, some trolls used to creep into the bedrooms of sleeping children. *Tan-Verk-Trollet,* the tiny toothache troll, was especially good at this trick. He would walk under a closed door and scamper over to each bed looking for a youngster who hadn't brushed his or her teeth. When he found one, he would dig a hole in a tooth and live there.

Naturally, not all Norwegian folk stories are quite so horrible. There are hundreds of other tales that children like to hear, such as "The Princess on the Glass Hill," "Taper Tom," and "The Lad and the North Wind." Some of these were collected by two young Norwegians, Peter Asbjørnsen and Jorgen Moe, who traveled around Norway. They eventually wrote a book about their adventures and the stories they uncovered.

The Vikings, however, liked their legends full of storm and fury. The old Norse literary works, called *sagas,* often were long poems that described the heroic activities of a king or a mighty chief. The sagas were written between the eleventh and fourteenth centuries. Before that they probably were oral works told by skalds. Some of the famous sagas tell of explorations to Iceland and Greenland, battles, and family histories.

LITERATURE AND THE THEATER

Norway's excellent modern writers have used many of the same themes in their works, drawing on all the colorful tales from the past. Knut Hamsun (1859-1952) and Sigrid Undset (1882-1949) won Nobel Prizes in literature for their excellent works. More recent history, including the period of the Nazi occupation of Norway, has been used by such writers as Tarjei Vessas.

Henrik Ibsen, Norway's most notable literary figure, wrote a marvelous play called *Peer Gynt* in 1857. Troll kings and other fantastic creatures confronted Ibsen's hero. The play is so popular even today that there is a Peer Gynt Road running through the mountains west of the Gudbrandsdal. The fictional Peer spent a lot of his time there. Ibsen himself, through his plays, changed the face of the theater of his day by emphasizing characters rather than plot. He had many imitators all over the world.

Some other fine Norwegian playwrights are Bjørnstjerne Bjørnson (1832-1910), Gunnar Heibeg (1857-1929), Nordahl Grieg (1902-1943), and Helge Krog (1889-1962). There are many professional theater companies in Norway, including a state-financed touring troupe, the Riksteatret. It takes excellent productions to small communities that don't have their own acting groups.

FILM

Unlike the films of Sweden and Denmark, Norway's motion pictures have not generally been shown outside the country, though their quality is very high. But during the 1970s, a group of young filmmakers made many excellent movies that were well-received around the world. Knut Anderson's *Scorched Earth* and *Under a Barren Sky* are good examples of this. Arnljot Berg, Paal Lokkeberg, and Anja Breien also have introduced fresh ideas into the country's film production. The government is liberal with grants to help pay for the work these artists are doing. Ten to

Edvard Grieg composed some of his music in this hut at Trollhaugen.

twelve movies are made each year by Norwegians. In addition, foreign producers often use the country as a locale for their films.

MUSIC

Next to literature and the theater, music is an important part of Norwegian culture. Even the Vikings enjoyed music played on horns and other crude instruments. Centuries-old folk dances with lively tunes are accompanied by the Hardanger fiddle, an instrument peculiar to Norway. Ole Bull (1810-1880) was a master violinist who often toured Europe and the United States. He played classical as well as folk music to huge audiences.

Edvard Grieg (1843-1907) is probably the best-known Norwegian composer. He wanted to show the importance of folk music and often incorporated it into his works. One of his best compositions was "In the Hall of the Mountain King." Most of his writings were for the piano, but he composed songs as well.

ART

Norwegian painting is dominated by the works of Edvard Munch (1863-1944). He produced a tremendous amount of work, ranging from paintings to a wall mural for a chocolate factory. Many of his pieces are sad and gloomy, perhaps because he was often ill and preferred to live alone. But he was an excellent painter and loved Norway.

Sculpture has a long history in Norway, beginning with Stone Age carvings on cliffs. Vikings carved wood for their ships and houses, using animal heads as subjects. Many excellent carvings adorn old churches. Gustav Vigeland (1869-1943) was lucky enough and talented enough to be asked to create outdoor art for an entire park in Oslo, with numerous statues, pillars, decorated gates, and bridges. Other well-known Norwegian sculptors of today are Nils Flakstad, Kaare Orud, Anne Raknes, Odd Hilt, and Kristopher Leirdal.

ARTS AND CRAFTS

There are many talented artisans and craft workers in Norway. Because the long winters lend themselves to hobbies, a Norwegian sometimes likes to cozy up in a warm kitchen and carve, paint, or weave. One of the best-known crafts is *rose maaling,* or rose painting. Each district has a distinctive rose-maaling style. Farmers used to paint their walls and furniture with swirls of bright flowers. Now artists use the technique on a wide variety of utensils and other items.

Jewelry making traditionally has been a Norwegian specialty. After all, the Vikings were excellent goldsmiths who made highly decorative bracelets and necklaces. Sometimes they would just break off a piece in payment for goods or services. Handmade silver buttons adorn the clothing of many farmers. These are products of long hours over a workbench. Some of the major jewelry-making firms have been in existence for at least two hundred years, with a father-to-son tradition of handing down quality service and products.

Another unusual art is the production of postage stamps. Famous Norwegians, landscapes, folktales, ships, and other subjects are used by the stamp designers. Some variations on the country's oldest stamps, dating from the 1850s, are very rare and valuable.

Norwegian artists use the technique of rose maaling (above) on a wide variety of items.

Norwegians retain a healthy respect for their artists, composers, designers, writers, and storytellers. This has been a national habit for generations.

The Norwegians are deeply reflective people, fashioned by their beautiful countryside—the pine forests, the peaks, and the ocean waves. No wonder they have produced generations of excellent thinkers, diplomats, artists, workers, sailors, and explorers. Their habits and mannerisms, their traditions, their friendliness, and their introspection are proof that Norway is certainly a land of enchantment.

Lowercase letters refer to map inserts.
An asterisk (*) refers to the approximate location of a place that does not appear on the map.

Ålesund	F2	Lofoten Islands	C5
And Fjord	C7	Mandal	H2
Andøya, island	C6	Molde	F2
Arendal	H3	Mosjøen	E5
Arnøya, island	B9	Moss	H4, p28
Berents Sea	A11	Mysen	p29
Berg	q27	Namsos	E4
Bergen	G1	Narvik	C7
Bodø	D6	North Cape	B11
Drammen	H4, p28	North Sea	I, J2
Egersund	H2	Norwegian Sea	E4
Eidsberg	H4, p29	Notodden	H3
Eidsvoll	G4	Numedal, valley	*G3
Elverum	G4	Odda	G2
Farsund	H2	Oppdal	F3
Finnmark	*B13	Oslo	G4, p28
Flekkefjord	H2	Oslo Fjord	H4, p28
Fredrikstad	H4, p28	Osterdal, valley	*G4
Frøya, island	F3	Porsangen Fjord	B11
Geiranger Fjord	*F2	Porsgrunn	p27
Gjøvik	G4	Rena	*G4
Glåma, river	G4	Ringvassøya, island	C8
Glittertinden, mountain	G3	Rjukan	H3
Grimstad	H3	Rogaland, county	*H1
Gudbrandsdal, valley	*G3	Rolvsøja, island	B10
Halden	H4	Romsdal	*F3
Hallingdal, valley	*G3	Sandefjord	p28
Hamar	G4	Sandnes	H1
Hammerfest	B10	Sarpsborg	p29
Hardanger Fjord	H1	Sauda	H2
Harstad	C7	Skien	H3, p27
Haugesund	H1	Smøla, island	F2
Hinnøya, island	C6	Snøhetta, mountain	F3
Hitra, island	F3	Sogne Fjord	G1
Horten	H4, p28	Sorlandet, region	*H2
Hvittingfoss	p28	Sørøya, island	B10
Jiek'kevarri, mountain	C8	Stavanger	H1
Jostedal Glacier	G2	Stokke	p28
Jotunheimen Range, mountains	G2	Tana Fjord	B13
Kongsberg	H3	Telemark, county	*H3
Kongsvinger	G4	Tønsberg	H4, p28
Kristiansand	H2	Tromsø	C8
Kristiansund	F2	Trondelag, county	*F4
Lake Femund (Femunden)	F4	Trondheim	F4
Lake Myøsa	G4	Trondheim Fjord	F3
Lakse Fjord	B12	Trysil	G5
Langesund	H3, p27	Vadsø	B13
Langøya, island	C6	Vardø	B14
Lapland, region	C12	Valdres, valley	*G3
Larvik	H4, p28	Varanger Fjord	B13
Leka, island	E4	Vega, island	E4
Lillehammer	G4	Vesterålen, archipelago	C6
Lista Fjord	H2	Vest Fjord	D5

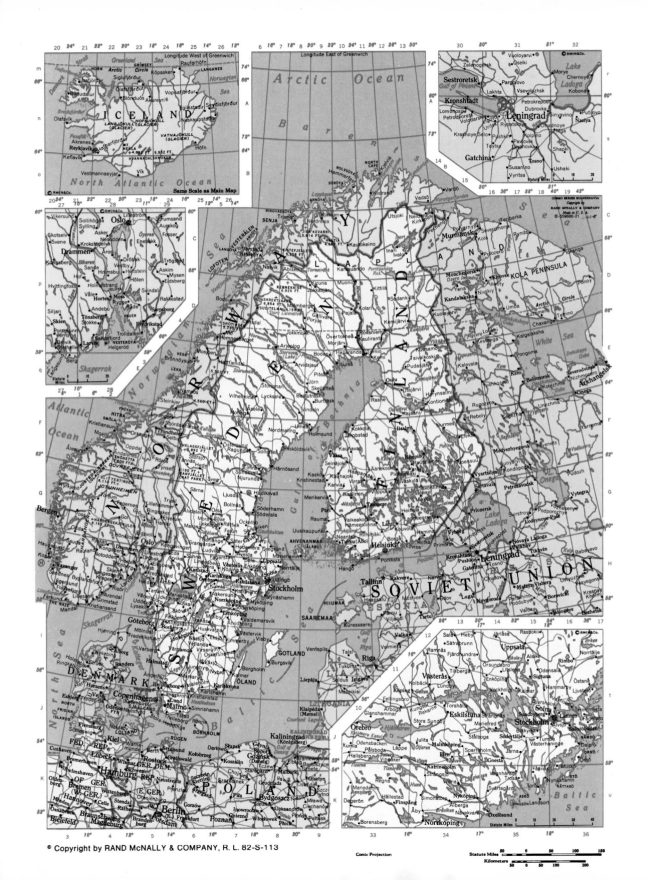

Conic Projection

Statute Miles

Kilometers

MINI-FACTS AT A GLANCE

GENERAL INFORMATION

Official Name: Kongeriket Norge (Norwegian); Kingdom of Norway

Capital: Oslo

Official Language: Norwegian. There are two forms—*Bokmaal* and *Nynorsk. Bokmaal* is used in most cities, towns, and schools.

Other Languages: Lapps speak their own language.

Government: Norway is a constitutional monarchy. The king is the head of state. The prime minister is the head of the government. The parliament, called the *Storting,* has 165 members who are elected to four-year terms. All citizens over the age of eighteen may vote. The government is divided into three branches: the executive, judicial, and legislative. The ombudsman is a government official who investigates complaints from citizens. The current government is based on the constitution of 1814.

Flag: The national flag has a large blue cross outlined in white on a red background.

Coat of Arms: The coat of arms features a lion, an ax, and the crown of St. Olav.

National Song: *"Ja vi elsker dette landet"* ("Yes, We Love with Fond Devotion This Land")

Religion: The official church is the Evangelical Lutheran Church. About 88 percent of the people belong to this church. Because there is religious freedom, people may join any church.

Money: Krone and øre. The plural of krone is kroner. There are 100 øre to the krone. Coins are 5, 10, 25, and 50 øre, and 1 and 5 kroner. Paper bills are 10, 50, 100, 500, and 1,000 kroner. In April 1996, 6.41 kroner were worth one dollar in United States currency.

Weights and Measures: Norway uses the metric system

Population: 4,382,000 (1996 estimate)

Cities: Most of the people live in the country's 450 or so municipalities. The largest of these are near the coastline:

Oslo	477,781
Bergen	219,884
Trondheim	142,188
Stavanger	102,637
Baerum	94,160
Kristiansund	67,863
Fredrikstad	64,843
Tromsø	54,503
Drammen	52,503

(Population figures based on 1994 estimates)

114

GEOGRAPHY

Highest Point: Glittertinden, 8,104 ft. (2,470 m)

Lowest Point: Sea level along the coast

Coastline: About 1,650 mi. (2,655 km), not including fjords and bays; about 15,000 mi. (24,000 km) including fjords, bays, and peninsulas

Rivers: The longest river in Norway is the Glåma, 380mi. (611.4 km) long.

Fjords: The longest fjord in Norway is Sogne Fjord, more than 100 mi. (161 km) long.

Mountains: Norway has many glacier-carved mountains. The highest mountain, Glittertinden, is in the Jotunheimen mountain range. It is the highest mountain in Europe north of the Alps. Most of Norway's highest mountains are in the south.

Glaciers: Norway has hundreds of glaciers. The Jostedal Glacier (300 sq. mi./777 km^2) is one of the largest ice fields in Europe.

Climate: Although Norway is often thought of as a cold and snowy country, it has a mild climate for a country that is far to the north. The mean temperature in Oslo in January is 24° F. (-4.4° C.). In July, the mean temperature in that city is 63° F. (17.2° C.). In winter, inland areas are colder than coastal areas. In summer, coastal areas are cooler than inland areas. In the north, there is sunshine twenty-four hours a day from May through July. There is no sunshine from the end of November to the end of January, but the aurora borealis can be seen.

Greatest Distances: Northeast to southwest—1,100 mi. (1,770 km)
Northwest to southwest—280 mi. (451 km)

Area: 125,182 sq. mi. (324, 221 km^2), not including the 24,208 sq. mi. (62,700 km^2) area of Svalbard, an Arctic archipelago that is part of Norway

NATURE

Trees: Common trees include spruce, fir, pine, oak, ash, beech, birch, elm, and willow. Logging is important to Norway. About 335 million cu. ft. (9,480.5 million m^3) of timber is cut each year. More than 12,000 mi. (19,308 km) of roads are used to transport logs. Logs are also transported down the country's many rivers.

Fish, coastal: Cod, herring, mackerel, haddock, capelin

Fish, inland: Salmon, trout

Animals: Common animals include the reindeer, elk, bear, badger, fox, lynx, and otter, as well as domestic animals. The wolf and the polar bear are endangered species.

EVERYDAY LIFE

Food: A typical Norwegian dinner consists of soup, meat or fish, potatoes, vegetables, and dessert. Dinner is eaten by city dwellers in late evening and by farm families at noon. Breakfast includes cereal and bread with cheese or jelly. Open-faced sandwiches are eaten at lunch and at late-evening supper. Farm families may eat as many as five meals a day and city families eat four meals a day.

Homes: Most housing in Norway has been built since the end of World War II. Many Norwegians live in apartment blocks, though about half the families in the country own their own homes.

Holidays:
>   January 1, New Year's Day
>   Holy Thursday
>   Good Friday
>   Easter Sunday
>   Easter Monday
>   Ascension
>   Whitmonday
>   May 1, Labor Day
>   May 17, Constitution Day (*Syttende Mai*)
>   June 24, St. John's Day
>   July 29, St. Olav's Day
>   October 24, United Nations Day
>   December 24, 25, and 26, Christmas

Culture: The Oslo University Library, with nearly 1.5 million books, is the largest library in the country. According to law, every city and town must have a free library. A special library service provides books to fishermen. There are natural history museums in Oslo, Stavanger, Trondheim, and Tromsø. Oslo and Bergen have large art collections. A traveling art gallery takes art exhibits to other areas. A collection of Viking ships is on exhibit in Oslo. That city also has a park created by sculptor Gustav Vigeland.

Recreation: Norwegians enjoy being outdoors. They especially love to ski, hike, sail, and swim.

Sports: Skiing is Norway's most popular sport. Ice skating is nearly as popular as skiing, with soccer, mountain climbing, hockey, and gymnastics not far behind.

Communications: Of the more than 2,000 newspapers in Norway, about 62 are published daily. There are also numerous trade journals and magazines, including 80 or so weekly magazines. The government owns the radio and television stations and everyone who owns a radio or television set must pay a yearly license fee for each set.

Transportation: There are more than 55,388 mi. (89,135 km) of roads in Norway. Many of these are paved with gravel. About 2 million private cars and 23,000 buses are registered. The government owns most of the railroads. For the state railway line, 775 tunnels, 3,000 bridges, and about 2,700 mi. (4,344 km) of track were constructed. About 80 percent of the trains are electric. The rest are diesel operated. Waterways also serve as transportation routes. Ferries carry people and timber down the fiords. There are 57 airports able to handle international flights. They are served by three airlines: the Braathens SAFE, the Scandinavian Airlines System (SAS), and the Wideroe Airline Company. The government owns Norwegian Airlines (DNL), which forms part of the SAS system. Another 20 airports accommodate smaller planes.

Schools: Every child between the ages of seven and sixteen must attend school. There are more than 3,500 primary schools in Norway, with nearly 470,000 students. The 1,000 or so secondary schools have an enrollment of about 180,000. There are more than 203 universities, colleges, and vocational schools, with an enrollment of nearly 73,675. Universities are located in Oslo, Bergen, Trondheim, and Tromsø. Almost every Norwegian can read and write.

Health: Norwegians are very healthy people. The infant mortality rate at 5 per 1,000 live births is one of the lowest in the world and the life expectancy rate at 74 years for males and 80 years for females is one of the highest. National health insurance provides free medical care.

Social Welfare: A compulsory National Insurance Scheme covers old age, disability, children, single parents, widowed spouses, sickness, maternity, adoption, and rehabilitation. The scheme provides a basic pension, and in some cases additional pensions. About one-third of the GDP is spent on social welfare annually.

Principal Products:
Agriculture: Livestock, dairy products, wheat, oats, rye, potatoes, barley, vegetables, fruit
Fishing: Cod, herring, capelin
Manufacturing: Chemicals, aluminum, magnesium, processed foods, wood pulp, paper
Energy: Petroleum
Mining: Iron ore, pyrites, ilmenite, lead, zinc, copper

VIKING LIFE

Food: The Vikings ate only two meals a day. Their diet included cheese; butter; oatmeal cakes and bread made from rye and oats; porridge made from oatmeal, barley, eggs, and honey; boiled, roasted, or stewed meat; fish; and a few fruits and vegetables. They drank milk, ale, and mead.

Houses: Average families lived in one-room houses made of wattle and mud. Wealthy people had large wooden longhouses, each with a long, rectangular hall. Inside the homes it was dark and plain. The Vikings used very little furniture.

Clothes: Men of average wealth wore long shirts, short, baggy pants, and a cloak. Wealthy men wore long pants, shirts, tunics, and fancy cloaks. Women wore long dresses and shawls. The shawls were fastened with two brooches connected by a chain. Married women wore their hair up in a knot.

Way of Life: The Vikings farmed, hunted, fished, made tools, repaired buildings, built boats; and raised sheep, cattle, and goats. In early spring, Viking seamen left in their *karfi* (warships) for their yearly raids overseas and did not return until fall.

IMPORTANT DATES

800—Vikings invade the British Isles

836—Vikings conquer Dublin

874—Iceland becomes a Viking colony

876—Vikings settle in France

900—Norway united by Harald Fair Hair (Harald I)

985—Greenland colonized by Eric the Red

995—Christianity introduced by Olav Tryggvason (Olav I)

998—Trondheim founded

1000—Leif Ericson sails to North America

1031—Olav Haraldson (Olav II) made patron saint of Norway

1036—The Irish under Brian Boru defeat the Viking armies

1048—Oslo founded

1066—Harald Hardrade (Harald III) killed in the Battle of Stamford Bridge

1070—Bergen founded

1240—Haakon the Old (Haakon IV) ends a long series of civil wars

1280—Norwegian coat of arms adopted

1349-50—The plague strikes Norway

1380—Denmark and Norway united

1397—Sweden joins the union with Denmark and Norway

1523—Sweden breaks away from the union with Denmark and Norway

1536—Norway becomes a Danish province; the Lutheran Church becomes the official church of Norway

1807—Trade with Britain suspended during Napoleonic Wars; many Norwegians starve

1811—University of Oslo founded

1814—Norway becomes part of Sweden under the Treaty of Kiel, Norway's present constitution adopted

1816—Bank of Norway founded

1845—Public assistance made available

1861—Norwegian Confederation of Sport founded

1884—Parliamentary rule introduced

1885—Two political parties established: the Liberal Party and the Conservative Party

1887—Workers form the Labor Party

1894—Government provides accident insurance for factory workers

1898—Present official flag adopted

1899—Norwegian Federation of Unions founded

1905—Norway becomes an independent nation; Haakon VII, a Danish prince, becomes Norway's king

1908—Accident insurance for fishermen becomes available

1913—Women win the right to vote

1914-1918—Norway neutral during World War I

1939—The Christian People's Party founded

1940—Germany invades Norway

1945—German troops withdraw from Norway

1946—Trygve Lie becomes the first secretary-general of the United Nations

1948—University of Bergen founded

1949—Norway becomes a member of the North Atlantic Treaty Organization

1952—Norway hosts the Winter Olympics

1956—A law allows women to become pastors in the Evangelical Lutheran Church

1959—Norway becomes a member of the European Free Trade Association

1960—Television broadcasting begins

1963—Norwegian Peace Corps established to help poor nations

1966—National Insurance Act establishes a new welfare program

1972—Norwegian voters decide not to join the European Economic Community (Common Market)

1989—In the largest aviation disaster in its history, 55 shipbuilders are killed in a chartered plane crash

1991—Harald V becomes king

1992—Norway applies to join the European Community (EC) and says that it will no longer seek to keep the value of the krone tied to the European monetary system

1993—Norway lifts trade and investment sanctions against South Africa; Gro Harlem Brundtland starts her fourth term as prime minister; Norway defies ban on hunting whales in the Antarctic that is imposed by the International Whaling Commission and kills 157 minke whales amidst protests from environmentalists

1994—Johan Jorgen Holst, who was instrumental in negotiating the PLO-Israeli framework to the accord on Palestinian self-rule, dies; Norwegian voters reject their nation's entry to the European Union (EU); Norway hosts the 17th Winter Olympic Games at Lillehammer, and wins 10 gold, 11 silver, and 5 bronze medals—the highest number of total medals won by any country; petroleum production reaches a record level of more than 2.7 million barrels per day

1995—Norway ends the moratorium (imposed in 1989) on the hunting of seal pups

IMPORTANT PEOPLE

Niels Henrik Abel (1802-29), mathematician, born in Findo

Roald Amundsen (1872-1928), explorer, born in Borge

Peter Christen Asbjørnsen (1812-85), writer and naturalist

Bernt Balchen (1899-1973), aviation pioneer, born in Tviet, near Arendal

Vilhelm Bjerknes (1862-1951), physicist

Bjørnstjerne Bjørnson (1832-1910), poet, playwright, and novelist, born near Trondheim

Johan Bojer (1872-1959), novelist and playwright

Ole Bornemann Bull (1810-80), composer and violinist, born in Bergen

Gro Harlem Brundtland (1939-   ), leader of the Labor Party; she won her fourth term as prime minister in 1993

Camilla Wergeland Collett (1813-95), novelist and pioneer for women's rights

Eric the Red (late 10th century), navigator who explored Greenland

Leif Ericson (late 10th century-early 11th century), son of Eric the Red, mariner and explorer who discovered North America about A.D. 1000.

Kirsten Flagstad (1895-1962), operatic soprano who became director of the Norwegian State Opera, born at Hamar

Ragnar Frisch (1895-1973), economist, shared the 1969 Nobel Prize in economics with Jan Tinbergen of The Netherlands, born in Oslo

Edvard Hagerup Grieg (1843-1907), composer, born in Bergen

Knut Hamsun (1859-1952), writer, winner of the 1920 Nobel Prize in literature, born at Loni

Armauer Gerhard Henrik Hansen (1841-1912), physician, discovered the cause of leprosy (Hansen's disease)

Christopher Hansteen (1784-1873), astronomer and physicist, researched terrestrial magnetism, born in Oslo

Odd Hassel, chemist, shared the 1969 Nobel Prize in chemistry with H.R. Barton of England

Sonja Henie (1913-69), figure skater and actress, Olympic gold medalist in figure skating in 1928, 1932, 1936

Thor Heyerdahl (1914-   ), explorer, born at Larvik

Henrik Ibsen (1828-1906), poet and dramatist, born in Skien

Alexander Lange Kielland (1849-1906), novelist and playwright, born in Stavanger

Christian Krohg (1852-1925), painter and writer

Christian Louis Lange (1869-1938), pacifist and historian, shared the 1921 Nobel Peace Prize with Hjalmar Branting of Sweden

Jonas Lie (1833-1908), writer

Trygve Halvdan Lie (1896-1968), politician, first secretary-general of the United Nations, born in Oslo

Edvard Munch (1863-1944), artist, born in Løton

Fridtjof Nansen (1861-1930), arctic explorer, naturalist, and statesman, winner of 1922 Nobel Peace Prize, born near Oslo

Vidkun A.L. Quisling (1887-1945), politician, collaborated in German conquest of Norway during World War II; his name has become a synonym for "traitor"

Johan Svendsen (1840-1911), composer

Liv Ullmann (1938-   ), actress

Sigrid Undset (1882-1949), writer, winner of the 1928 Nobel Prize in literature, born in Kallundborg, Denmark, raised in Olso

Fartein Olav Valen (1887-1952), composer

Gustav Vigeland (1869-1943), sculptor, created Frogner Park in Oslo

Erik Werenskiold (1855-1938), painter and illustrator

Henrik Arnold Wergeland (1808-1845), poet, dramatist, editor and patriot; brother of Camilla Collett

RULERS OF NORWAY

The Vikings (900-1380)	Reign
Harald Fair Hair (Harald I)	872-940
Erik Bloody Axe (Erik I)	940-945
Haakon the Good (Haakon I)	945-960
Harald II	960-970
Earl Haakon	970-995
Olav Tryggvason (Olav I)	995-1000
Earls Erik and Svein	1000-1016
Olav Haraldson (St. Olav, Olav II)	1016-1028
Canute the Great (Prince Svein Alfivason, regent)	1028-1035
Magnus the Good (Magnus I)	1035-1047
Harald Hardrade (Harald III)	1047-1066
Magnus II and Olav the Peaceful (joint rule)	1066-1069
Olav the Peaceful (Olav III)	1069-1093

Magnus Bareleg (Magnus III)	1093-1103
Eystein Magnusson (Eystein I)	1103-1125
Sigurd Magnusson the Crusader (Sigurd I)	1125-1130
Harald Gilchrist (Harald IV)	1130-1136
Magnus Sigurdson the Blind (Magnus IV)	1136-1138
Sigurd II and Inge I (joint rule)	1138-1155
Inge I	1155-1161
Magnus V	1162-1179
Eystein Haraldson (Eystein II) — rival claim	1142-1157
Haakon Sigurdson (Haakon II) — rival claim	1161-1162
Magnus Erlingson (Magnus V)	1179-1184
Sverre Sigurdson	1184-1202
Haakon Haakonson (Haakon III)	1202-1204
Inge Baardson (Inge II)	1204-1217
Haakon the Old (Haakon IV)	1217-1263
Magnus the Lawmaker (Magnus VI)	1263-1280
Eric the Priest Hater (Eric II)	1280-1299
Haakon Magnusson (Haakon V)	1299-1319
Magnus Erikson (Magnus VII)	1319-1355
Haakon Magnusson (Haakon VI)	1355-1380

Rulers of Denmark and Norway (1380-1814)

	Reign
Olav Haakonson (Olav IV)	1380-1387
Queen Margaret	1387-1412
Erik of Pomerania (Erik III)	1389-1442
Christopher of Bavaria	1442-1448
Christian I	1448-1481
Hans	1481-1513
Christian the Cruel (Christian II)	1513-1523
Frederik I	1523-1533
Christian III	1535-1559
Frederik II	1559-1588
Christian IV	1588-1648
Frederik III	1648-1670
Christian V	1670-1699
Frederik IV	1699-1730
Christian VI	1730-1746
Frederik V	1746-1766
Christian VII	1766-1808
Frederik VI	1808-1814
Christian Frederik (king of Norway May 17-November 4, 1814)	

Kings of Sweden and Norway (1814-1905)

Carl XIII	1814-1818
Carl XIV (Bernadotte)	1818-1844
Oscar I	1844-1859
Carl XV	1859-1872
Oscar II	1872-1905

Kings of Norway (1905 to present)

Haakon VII	1905-1957
Olav V	1957-1991
Harald V	1991-

INDEX

Page numbers that appear in boldface type indicate illustrations

Abel, Niels Henrik, 103, 120
aeser (good gods), 11
Agricultural Museum, Bergen, 65
agriculture, **38**, 39, 53, **90,** 91
airlines, 98, 116
akevitt (liquor), 51
Amnesty International, 100
Amundsen, Roald, **102**, 103, 120
Anderson, Knut, 107
animals, 71, 115
Antarctic territories, 55
Arabia, 8
Arctic, 100, 101
Arctic Cathedral, Tromsø, **48**
Arctic Circle, 54, 55, 66, 68
Arctic Ocean, 103

area, 115
art, 109,110
Asbjørnsen, Peter, 106, 120
Astrid (Princess), 80
Barton, Derek H. R., 99
Bear Island, 55
Berg, Arnljot, 107
Bergen, 21, **21**, 64, **64**, 65, 89, 114, 118
Billy Goats Gruff, 105
"Birch Legs," 75
birds, **70**, 71
Bjørnson, Bjørnstjerne, 107, 120
Bjørnsund, 43
Black Plague, 22, 118
Black Sea, 8, 12
"blue meadow," **34**, 35

boat transportation, 69, 116
Bokmaal ("book language"), 37, 114
Bonnevie, Margaret, 87
borders, 55
Borgund, 22
Bouvet Island, 55
Breien, Anja, 107
Brian Boru, 14, **14**, 118
Briksdal Glacier, **73**
Britain, 7, 16, 21, 118
Bronze Age people, 10
Bull, Ole, 109, 120
Camp Norway, 43
capital, 20, 22, 56, 83, 114
Carl XIII, 27
Carl XIV, 61

Carl, Prince of Denmark (Haakon VII), 29, **29**, 30, 31, 33, 44, 82, 119
Caroline Institute, Sweden, 99
cathedrals, 22, **48**, **49**, 80, 81
Catholic church, 22, 47
children, 40, 41, 43, 87, 88, **88**, 116
Christian Frederik (King), 24-27, **26**
Christianity, 19, 44, 47, 118
Christmas, 45, **45**, 46
chronology, 118, 119
churches, 22, **23**, 47, **48**, **49**, 56, 80, 81
cities, major, 114
climate, 66, 67, 115
Clontarf, Ireland, 14
coastline, 51, 115
coat of arms, 114, 118
codfish drying racks, 71, **72**
Collett, Camilla, 87, 120
Columbus, Christopher, 15
communications, 98, 116
constitution, 25-27, 43, 46, 81-83, 114, 119
constitution, writers of, 25, **25**
cooperative movement, 86
council of state (Statsraad), 81
crafts, 110
crops, 91
culture, 116
dancing, 40, **40**
dates, important, 118, 119
daylight, twenty-four-hour, 66, 67, 115
Denmark, 12, 16, 19, 20, 22, 24, 27, 29, 39, 80, 107, 118
depression (1930s), 30, 86
distances, greatest, 55, 115
dragon ships, 7, 8
Drammen, 114
Dublin, Ireland, 14, 118
E6 highway, 68
education, 76, 87-89, 116
Eidsvoll, 25, 43, 69, 97
electricity, 96

emigrants, 27, 64
England, 19, 20, 24, 31
environmental protection, 73
Equal Status Act, 87
Erik Bloody Axe, 18
Eric the Red, 15, 118, 120
Eskimos, 15
ethnic groups, 36
Evangelical Lutheran Church, 46-47, 114, 119
explorers, 56, 100-103
explorers, Viking, 13, 15
exports, 97
Faeroe Islands, 18
farming, **38**, 39, 53, **90**, 91
Ferkingstad, 43
Ferner, Johan Martin, 80
ferryboats, 68, 69, **69**
figureheads, 16, **16**
figure skating, 78
Finland, 33, 55
Finnmark, 33, 36, 66, 67, 68
fires, 56, 64
fish and fishing, 21, 30, 39, 50, 51, 71, 72, **72**, 93-95, **94**, 115
fish market, Bergen, 64, **64**
fjords, 53, 56, **60**, 61, 63, **63**, 68, **69**, **93**, 115
flag, 114, 119
Flagstad, Kirsten, 103, 120
Flakstad, Nils, 110
folk schools, 89
folktales, 104-106
food, 46, 50, 51, 115, 117
forestry, 92, **92**
forests, **28**, 61, 72, 92
Foss, 55
Fram (ship), 101, **101**, 103
France, 14, 20, 24, 30, 118
Frisch, Ragnar, 99, 120
fruit, 66, 91
gas, 96
Geiranger Fjord, **63**
geography, 53, 115
Germany, 30-33, 119
Gestapo, 33
Gibraltar, Strait of, 12

glaciers, 53, 54, **73**, 115
Glåma River, 61, 115
Glittertinden, 115
gnomes, 105, **105**
gods, 11, **11**, 19, 75
government, 81-83, 114
Great Britain, 30, 80, 92
Greenland, 13, 15, **15**, 18, 101, 106, 118
Grieg, Edvard, 109, 120
Grieg, Nordahl, 107
Grieg's hut, Trollhaugen, **108**
Gudbrandsdal, 75, 107
Gudbrandsdal Valley, 62
Haakon IV, 22, 118
Haakon V, 22
Haakon VII, 29, **29**, 30, 31, 33, 44, 82, 119
Haakon Haakonson, 75
Haakon Magnus (Prince), 80
Haakon the Longbeard, 7
Hallingdal, 70
Hallingdal Valley, 62, **62**
Hammerfest, 54, 72
Hamsun, Knut, 106, 120
handicapped, sports program, 77, **77**
Hanseatic League, 21, 22, 65
Hansen, Armauer, 65, 120
Hansen's disease (leprosy), 65
Hansteen, Aasta, 87
Harald (Crown Prince), 80, 82
Harald Fair Hair, 18, 19, 21, 80, 118
Harald Gray Fur, 18
Harald Hardrade, 20, 21, 118
harbors, 54, **54**, **59**, 64, **64**
Hardanger fiddle, 109
Harold (King of England), 20, **20**
Hassel, Odd, 99, 120
Hastings, Battle of, 20
Haugesund, **6**, **95**
health and health care, 85, **85**, 117
Hebrides Islands, 18
Heibeg, Gunnar, 107
Henie, Sonja, 78, **78**, 120

Heyerdahl, Thor, 56, 103, 120
highest point, 115
Hilt, Odd, 110
Hitler, Adolf, 30, 31
holidays, 43-46, 116
Holmenkollen ski jump, 61, 76
homes, 35, 116
hotels, 69
hoyjellshotell (mountain resorts), 69
Ibsen, Henrik, 107, 120
Iceland, 8, 13, 15, 18, 106, 118
imports, 97
Independence Day (*Syttende Mai*), 26, 43, 79
International Labor Organization, 100
"In the Hall of the Mountain King," 109
Ireland, 8, 14, 18, 27
islands, 53, 55
Isle of Man, 18
Jan Mayen Island, 55
jewelry making, 110
Jostedal Glacier, 115
jotners (evil gods), 11
Jotunheimen range, 53, 115
Kamoy Island, 43
karfi (Viking warships), 7
Karl Johans Gate, Oslo, **42**, 61
Kaupang, 16
Kiel, Treaty of, 24, 27, 118
King, Martin Luther, Jr., 100
kings of Norway, list of, 122
Knut (King of Denmark and England), 19
Kon-Tiki (book), 103
Kon-Tiki (raft), 56, **102**
Kon-Tiki Museum, 56, 102
Kristiansand, 112
Kristiansund, 63, 112
Krog, Helge, 107
Labor Party, 84, 119
"Lad and the North Wind, The," 106
Laestadius, 48
Land of the Midnight Sun, 67

Land of the Strawberries, 66
languages, 37, 39, 114
Lapps, 18, 36, **36**, 37, **37**, 47, 48, **66**, 91, 114
League of Nations High Commissioner for Refugees, 100
Leirdal, Kristopher, 110
lemmings, 71
leprosy (Hansen's disease), 65
Leprosy Museum, Bergen, 65
libraries, 116
Lie, Trygve, 46, 119, 121
Lillehammer, 69, 75, 119
Lofoten Islands, 43, 93
Lokkeberg, Paal, 107
London, England, 31
Longyearbyen, 67
Lorentzen, Erling, 80
lowest point, 115
lutefisk (lye fish), 50
Lutheran Church, 22, 46-47, 114, 118, 119
Magnus III (Magnus Bareleg), 21
Magnus IV (Magnus the Lawmaker), 22
Magnus II (son of Harald Hardrade), 21
Magnus the Blind, 18
Mandel, 62
maps of Norway:
  ancient kingdom, **18**
  political map, **113**
  topography, **2**
  Europe, regional map, **1**
Maritime Museum, 101
maritime schools, 89
Marshall, George Catlett, 100
Marshall Plan, 33, 100
Martha (Princess), 80
Martha Louise (Princess), 80
Maud (Queen), 80
mead, 20
Mediterranean Sea, 12
merchant fleet, 95, 96
Middle Age, 56
midnight sun, 67

Midsummer Eve, 44
Ministry of Environment, 73
missionaries, 48
Moe, Jorgen, 106
Molde, 43
monarchy, 79-82
money, 114
motto, Olav V, 81
mountain climbing, 76
mountains, **52**, 53, 115
movies, 107
Munch, Edvard, 56, 109, 121
Municipal Art Museum, Bergen, 65
museums, 56, **57**, 61, 65, **65**, 95, 101, 102, 116
music, 104, 109
mythology, 10, 11, 75
Nansen, Fridtjof, 100, 101, **101**, 121
Napoleon, 24
Napoleonic Wars, 24, 118
Narvik, 104
National Federation of Unions, 86, 119
National Insurance System, 84
national parks, 73
Nazis, 30-33, 47, 62
Newfoundland, 15, 18
newspapers, 98, 116
Nidaros Cathedral, 81
nisse (elf), 46, 105
Nobel, Alfred, 99, 100
Nobel Peace Prize, 100
Nobel Prizes, 99, 100, 107
Nobile, Umberto, 103
Norge (dirigible), 103
Norge (royal yacht), 82
Normandy, France, 14
Normans, 20
Norsemen (see Vikings)
North America, 13, 15
North Atlantic Current, 54, 66, 93
North Pole, 103
North Sea, 16, 96
Norway, derivation of word, 53

Norwegian-American Cultural Institute, 43
Norwegian Association for Women's Rights, 87
Norwegian Employers Confederation, 86
Norwegian International Ship Register (NIS), 96
Norwegian State Opera, 103
Numedal Valley, 62
Nusfjord, **93**
Nynorsk (New Norwegian language), 37, 114
Odin (god), 11, **11**
oil, 96
oil rig, **96**
Olav I (Olav Tryggvason), 19, **19**, 118
Olav II (Olav Haraldson), 19, **19**, 44, 118
Olav III (Olav the Peaceful), 21, 64
Olav V, 31, 33, 44, 79-82, **81**
Old Bergen Museum, **65**
Olympics, 78, 82
ombudsman, 83, 114
Orkneys, 18
Orud, Kaare, 110
Oscar II, 28
Oseberg dragon head, **16**
Oslo, 20, 22, 35, **42**, 44, 56, **57-60**, 61, 76, 78, 79, 80, 83, 89, 91, 97, 100, 101, 110, 114, 115, 116, 118
Oslo Cathedral, 80
Oslo City Hall (radhus), **59**
Oslo Fjord, 16, 56, **60**, 61, 95
Oslo Historical Museum, 56
Oslo Ship Museum, 56, **57**
Oslo University Library, 116
Osterdal, 75
outdoor life, 40, 41, **41**, 43, 75, 78, 116
parliament (Storting), 26, 27, 28, **58**, 61, 81-84, 87, 100, 114, 119
patron saint of Norway, 19, 44, 118
Peer Gynt, 107

people of Norway, 36
people of Norway, important, list of, 120, 121
Peter I Island, 55
plants, 72
playwrights, 107
polar bears, **70**
population figures, 27, 35, 36, 114
postage stamps, 110
potato farmers, **38**
"Princess on the Glass Hill, The," 106
products, principal, 117
Protestant church, 22
Queen Maud's Land, 55
Quisling, Vidkun, 31-33, **32**, 121
Radhus (Oslo City Hall), **59**
Ra Expeditions, The, 103
Ragnhild (Princess), 80
raids, Viking, 12, 14, 18
railroads, 97, **97**, **98**, 116
rainfall, 65, 68
Raknes, Anne, 110
recreation, 40, 116
Reformation, 22, 47
reindeer, 37, **37**, 66, **66**, 91
religion, 19, 22, 46-48, 114, 118, 119
Rena, 75
Riksteatret, 107
rivers, 61, 115
roads, 68, 116
rock carvings, 10, **10**, 109
Rogaland, 104
Roman Catholic church, 22, 47
Romsdal, 4
Roosevelt, Franklin D., 61
rose maaling, 110, **111**
Royal Academy of Science, Sweden, 99
royal family, 79-82, **81**
rulers of Norway, list of, 121, 122
Russia, 12, 30, 36, 55
sagas, 104, 106

St. Canute Feast Day, 46
St. Hans (John), festival, 43, 44
St. Olav's Day, 44
Saltfjell plateau, 68
Samis (Lapps), 36
Sandefjord, 95
Scandinavia, 12, 13, 36, 48, 105
schools, 76, 87-89, **88**, 96, 116
Scorched Earth, 107
Scotland, 18
sculpture, 109, 110
sea, importance to Norway, 13, **34**, 35, 51, 53, 89
"Seaman's Sports," 76
shaman (Lapp "priest"), 48
sheep, **70**
Shetland Islands, 18
shipping, 95, 96
ships, Viking, 7-9, **9**, 10, **10**, 12, **12**, 16, 56, **57**, 95, 116
shipyard, Haugesund, **95**
Sigurd I, 21
Skade (ski goddess), 75
skalds (minstrels), 8, 10, 104, 106
Skibladner (paddle-wheel ship), 69
skiing, 61, 62, **74**, 75, 76, 77
skraelings (native Americans), 15
smorgasbord, **51**
snowfall, 68
social-welfare programs, 83-85, 119
Sogne Fjord, 115
song, national, 114
Sonja (Princess), **77**, 80
Sorlandet, 62
"South Land, The," 62
South Pole, 103
Soviet Union (see Russia)
Spain, 26
Spitzbergen (Svalbard) Island, 55
sports, 61, 62, 75-78, 82, 116
Stamford Bridge, Battle of, 20, 118
Statsraad (council of state), 81

statues, 61
Stavanger, 21, 63, 114
stave (wooden) churches, **23,** 47, 56
Stiklestad, Battle of, 44
Stockholm, Sweden, 27, 28, 99, 100
Stone Age, 10, 56, 109
Storting (parliament), 26, 27, 28, **58,** 61, 81-84, 87, 100, 114, 119
Stortorget (open market), **58,** 61
strawberries, 66
Svalbard (Spitzbergen) Island, 55, 67, 115
Sweden, 12, 16, 18, 24, 26, 27, 28, 31, 55, 80, 99, 100, 107, 118
Swedish Academy of Literature, 99
Syttende Mai (Independence Day), 26, 43, 79
"Taper Tom," 106
Telemark, 62
temperatures, 115
Thor (god), 11
thralls (slaves), 8, 36
timber, 28, 61, 92, **92,** 115
ting (governing council), 22
trade, 28, 30, 65, 118

trade, Viking, 16, 21
transportation, 68, 69, 97, 98, 116
trees, 72, 92, 115
Trollhaugen, 108
Troll Path (Trollstigen), Romsdal, **4**
trolls, 104-106, **105**
Tromsø, 48, 89
Trondelag, 65
Trondheim, 44, 89, 114, 118
Trondheim Cathedral, **49**
Trondheim Fjord, 65
Ull (ski god), 75
Ulster Annals, 14
Under a Barren Sky, 107
underground (World War II), 31, 33
Undset, Sigrid, 106, 121
United Nations Children's Fund (UNICEF), 100
United Nations Day, 46
United States of America, 26, 27, 33, 61, 83
universities, 76, 88, 89, 116, 118, 119
University of Trondheim, **89**
vacations, 41, 43, 78

Valdres Valley, 62
Valhalla, 11
Vessas, Tarjei, 107
Vigeland, Gustav, 109, 116, 121
Viking explorers, 13, 15
Viking raids, 12, 14, 18
Vikings, **5,** 7-20, **13, 16, 17,** 53, 56, 64, 65, 95, 104, 106, 109, 110, 117, 118, 121
Viking ships, 7-9, **9,** 10, **10,** 12, **12,** 16, 56, **57,** 95, 116
Viking trade, 16, 21
voting, 83, 87, 114, 119
waterfalls, 54, **55,** 63
weddings, 40
weights and measures, 114
welfare programs, 84, 119
Western Sea, **6,** 7
whaling, 95
"White Christ," 19
wild flowers, 72, **73**
women's rights, **86,** 87, 119
workers' rights, 86, 119
work habits, 39
World War I, 30, 119
World War II, 30-33, 47, 61, 62
writers, 106, 107

About the Author

Martin Hintz is one-quarter Norwegian, which might explain why he enjoys cross-country skiing. It's also the reason why he likes lutefisk, that smelly Norwegian cod. His family—wife Sandy, sons Daniel and Stephen, and daughter Kate—like to ski, too, but they just don't understand Hintz's appreciation of that famous Scandinavian seafood dish. As a young man, Hintz's great-grandfather, Louis A. Larson, emigrated to America from Bergen, Norway just before the turn of the century. Larson settled in Lawler, Iowa, where he opened a pioneer general store. Hintz still remembers going into the place when it was operated by his great-aunt. Hintz currently lives in Milwaukee, Wisconsin, and has nine books to his credit, ranging from one on the training and care of elephants to a cook book (one that doesn't mention lutefisk). A former newspaper reporter, Hintz has a master's degree in journalism.